MATTHEW
for
EVERYONE

PART 2
CHAPTERS 16-28

MATTHEW
for
EVERYONE

PART 2
CHAPTERS 16—28

TOM
WRIGHT

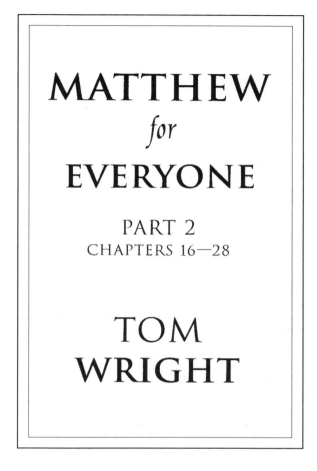

SPCK

Westminster John Knox Press

First published in Great Britain in 2002 by
Society for Promoting Christian Knowledge
36 Causton Street
London
SW1P 4ST

This second edition copublished in 2004 by the Society for Promoting
Christian Knowledge, London, and Westminster John Knox Press,
100 Witherspoon Street, Louisville, KY 40202.

07 08 09 10 11 12 13 — 10 9 8 7 6 5 4

British Library Cataloguing-in-Publication Data
A catalogue record for this book is available from the British Library.

ISBN 978–0–281–05487–9 (U.K. edition)

United States Library of Congress Cataloging-in-Publication Data is
on file at the Library of Congress, Washington, D.C.

ISBN 978–0–664–22787–6 (U.S. edition)

Typeset by Pioneer Associates, Perthshire
Printed in Great Britain at
Ashford Colour Press

Produced on paper from sustainable forests

CONTENTS

CONTENTS

For

Christopher Philip Unwin,

priest and teacher of the faith,
with gratitude for the love, support and prayers
of over fifty years

INTRODUCTION

On the very first occasion when someone stood up in public to tell people about Jesus, he made it very clear: this message is for *everyone*.

It was a great day – sometimes called the birthday of the church. The great wind of God's spirit had swept through Jesus' followers and filled them with a new joy and a sense of God's presence and power. Their leader, Peter, who only a few weeks before had been crying like a baby because he'd lied and cursed and denied even knowing Jesus, found himself on his feet explaining to a huge crowd that something had happened which had changed the world for ever. What God had done for him, Peter, he was beginning to do for the whole world: new life, forgiveness, new hope and power were opening up like spring flowers after a long winter. A new age had begun in which the living God was going to do new things in the world – beginning then and there with the individuals who were listening to him. 'This promise is for *you*,' he said, 'and for your children, and for everyone who is far away' (Acts 2.39). It wasn't just for the person standing next to you. It was for everyone.

Within a remarkably short time this came true to such an extent that the young movement spread throughout much of the known world. And one way in which the *everyone* promise worked out was through the writings of the early Christian leaders. These short works – mostly letters and stories about Jesus – were widely circulated and eagerly read. They were never intended for either a religious or intellectual elite. From the very beginning they were meant for everyone.

That is as true today as it was then. Of course, it matters that some people give time and care to the historical evidence, the meaning of the original words (the early Christians wrote in Greek), and the exact and particular force of what different writers were saying about God, Jesus, the world and themselves. This series is based quite closely on that sort of work. But the point of it all is that the message can get out to everyone, especially to people who wouldn't normally read a book with footnotes and Greek words in it. That's the sort of person for whom these books are written. And that's why there's a glossary, in the back, of the key words that you can't really get along without, with a simple description of what they mean. Whenever you see a word in **bold type** in the text, you can go to the back and remind yourself what's going on.

There are of course many translations of the New Testament available today. The one I offer here is designed for the same kind of reader: one who mightn't necessarily understand the more formal, sometimes even ponderous, tones of some of the standard ones. I have of course tried to keep as close to the original as I can. But my main aim has been to be sure that the words can speak not just to some people, but to everyone.

Matthew's gospel presents Jesus in a rich, many-sided way. He appears as the Messiah of Israel, the king who will rule and save the world. He comes before us as the teacher greater even than Moses. And, of course, he is presented as the son of man giving his life for us all. Matthew lays it all out step by step and invites us to learn the wisdom of the gospel message and the new way of life that results from it. So here it is: Matthew for everyone!

Tom Wright

PALESTINE
In New Testament
times

Tyre

•Caesarea
Philippi

SYRO-
PHOENICIA

SYRIA

•Ptolemais   Chorazin•   •Bethsaida
Capernaum•
Gennesaret• Sea of Galilee

MT CARMEL   Tiberias•   Gergesa?

Cana•
•Nazareth   •Gadara
•Nain

Plain
of Esdraelon

Mediterranean Sea

•Caesarea

Salim•
Aenon•

Samaria•   Gerasa•
SAMARIA
•Sychar

Plain of Sharon   ▲MT GERIZIM

•Antipatris

•Joppa   •Arimathea   Ephraim•

Lydda•

Jericho•
Emmaus•   •Bethany-
Jerusalem• •Bethphage   beyond-Jordan
JUDAEA   •Bethany
•Azotus   Qumran

River Jordan

•Askelon   Bethlehem•

Hebron•

Dead Sea

•Gaza   Wilderness of Judaea

IDUMEA   NABATAEA
•Beersheba

DECAPOLIS

MATTHEW 16.1–12

The Leaven of the Pharisees

¹The Pharisees and Sadducees came to Jesus and tried to catch him out by asking him to show them a sign from heaven.

²This was his reply to them: 'When it's evening you say, "It's going to be fine, because the sky is turning red." ³And in the morning you say, "It's going to be stormy today, because the sky is red and gloomy." Well then: you know how to work out the look of the sky, so why can't you work out the signs of the times? ⁴The generation that wants a sign is wicked and corrupt! No sign will be given to it, except the sign of Jonah.'

With that, he left them and went away.

⁵When the disciples crossed over the lake, they forgot to bring any bread. ⁶'Watch out,' said Jesus to them, 'and beware of the leaven of the Pharisees and Sadducees.'

⁷They discussed it with each other. 'It's because we didn't bring any bread,' they said.

⁸But Jesus knew what they were thinking.

'You really are a little-faith lot!' he said. 'Why are you discussing with each other that you haven't got any bread? ⁹Don't you understand, even now? Don't you remember the five loaves and the five thousand, and how many basketfuls you picked up afterwards? ¹⁰Or the seven loaves and the four thousand, and how many baskets you picked up? ¹¹Why can't you see that I wasn't talking about bread? Watch out for the leaven of the Pharisees and Sadducees!'

¹²Then they understood that he wasn't telling them to beware of the leaven you get in bread, but of the teaching of the Pharisees and Sadducees.

Our generation is bombarded with signs. Drive along a city street, especially at night, and your eyes will be dazzled with signs of all sorts. Some of them are necessary to tell you where to go and where not to go: if you ignore red and green lights you will be in danger. Others are merely for decoration and

1

information, pointing to particular buildings or illuminating them. Many others are designed to catch your imagination – and your money. Advertisements twinkle and flash enticingly until their message has worked its way into your memory.

Part of growing up is learning to distinguish signs that matter, which must be obeyed, from signs that don't matter, that can (and perhaps should) be ignored. Something of the same puzzle faces us as we read the **gospels**. Sometimes Jesus does things which he himself speaks of as 'signs'. Particularly in John's gospel, but also in the others, some of his powerful deeds, especially his healings, are seen as signs of who he is, signs that the **disciples** at least, and probably others as well, are meant to notice, to 'read', to understand.

But when the **Pharisees** and **Sadducees** ask for a sign, something different is going on. (They didn't normally work together; they must have regarded this as something of an emergency.) Matthew says they were trying to catch him out; it was a test, a trick. Perhaps they were wanting to accuse him again of being in league with the devil (see 12.24–45). Perhaps they were hoping to bring a charge against him that he was a false prophet, using signs and wonders to lead Israel astray, as the scriptures had warned (Deuteronomy 13.1–5). Perhaps Jesus saw their challenge as being like the cynicism of Israel in the wilderness, putting God to the test to see whether he was really among them or not (Exodus 17.1–7). In any case, Jesus refused to comply with the request. He would not perform signs to order, as though he had to pass some kind of test. To do so would be to treat God himself as a kind of circus performer.

Of course, Jesus was doing all sorts of 'signs'; the gospel story is full of them. And he longed for people to be able to read 'the signs of the times': to see the gathering storm-clouds in Israel's national life, to recognize the way in which corrupt leaders, false teachers, and people bent on violence were leading the nation towards inevitable disaster, from which only **repentance** and a fresh trust in God's **kingdom** could save them. The irony was that they were asking him for a sign, but they were blind to the many signs all around them.

So he refused to perform some special sign just for them. His powerful works were done from love, not from a desire to submit his mission to a laboratory test. They weren't that kind of thing. The only sign he would give such people, as he said before, was the sign of Jonah (12.38–42, where the meaning of this is spelled out). If people watched him with only cynicism and criticism in their hearts, they would see nothing – until the moment when the rumour went around that he had been raised from the dead. That would be the final and devastating sign that God had indeed been with him all along.

The truth of the matter, of course, was that both the Pharisees and the Sadducees, in their different ways, held aims, beliefs and hopes which were seriously out of line with those Jesus was offering. Like established political parties that suddenly become aware of a new movement threatening to undermine their support, they are ready to do anything they can to discredit it. But Jesus not only sees through their plot; he has his own warning to give against them.

Like a parent teaching a child not to be led astray by the flashy signs of city advertisements, he warns them of the 'leaven' of the Pharisees and Sadducees. This was puzzling to the disciples, who thought Jesus was referring cryptically to the fact that they'd forgotten to bring any bread with them. It is even more puzzling to us, because unless we have grown up knowing something about Judaism we probably don't know what leaven could stand for.

The point is this. At Passover, one of the greatest Jewish festivals, all leaven had to be cleared out of the house, commemorating the time when the children of Israel left Egypt in such a hurry that they didn't have time to bake leavened bread, and so ate it unleavened. Gradually, 'leaven' became a symbol

3

not for something that makes bread more palatable, but for something that makes it less pure. Warning against the 'leaven' of someone's teaching meant warning against ways in which the true message of God's kingdom could be corrupted, diluted, or (as we say, referring to drink rather than bread), 'watered down'.

Bring the whole scene forward two thousand years, and we face the question for ourselves. What are the 'signs of the times' in our own day? Where are leaders and teachers, official and unofficial, leading people astray? What are the true signs of God's work in our midst? How can we learn to tell the difference, in our moral and spiritual life together, between the signs we must observe and those we would do better to ignore?

MATTHEW 16.13–20

Peter's Declaration of Jesus' Messiahship

¹³Jesus came to Caesarea Philippi. There he put this question to his disciples:

'Who do people say that the son of man is?'

¹⁴'John the Baptist,' they replied. 'Others say Elijah. Others say Jeremiah, or one of the prophets.'

¹⁵'What about you?' he asked them. 'Who do you say I am?'

¹⁶Simon Peter answered.

'You're the Messiah,' he said. 'You're the son of the living God!'

¹⁷'God's blessing on you, Simon, son of John!' answered Jesus. 'Flesh and blood didn't reveal that to you; it was my father in heaven. ¹⁸And I've got something to tell you, too: you are Peter, the rock, and on this rock I will build my church, and the gates of hell won't overpower it. ¹⁹I will give you the keys of the kingdom of heaven. Whatever you tie up on earth will be tied up in heaven, and whatever you untie on earth will be untied in heaven.'

²⁰Then he sternly ordered the disciples not to tell anyone that he was the Messiah.

The Tibetan Buddhists believe in the transmigration of **souls**. When someone dies, they suppose that the soul of that person goes immediately into a different body, the body of a child born at the same instant.

This belief becomes vitally important when their spiritual leader, the Dalai Lama, dies. A search is made for a boy born at the moment when the great leader died; and that boy is taken away and brought up as the new leader. Everybody, including the person himself, knows from the very beginning that he is the new Dalai Lama. It sounds very strange to modern Western ears. We prize highly the right of every person to freedom of choice about their future. Even hereditary monarchs can abdicate. But the Dalai Lama has no choice; and there is no question about who he is.

In Judaism it was very different. Many Jews of Jesus' day believed (and many Jews today still believe this) that God would send an anointed king who would be the spearhead of the movement that would free Israel from oppression and bring justice and peace to the world at last. Nobody knew when or where this anointed king would be born, though many believed he would be a true descendant of King David. God had made wonderful promises about his future family. Some would have pointed to the prophecy of Micah 5.1–3 (which Matthew quotes in chapter 2) as indicating that the coming king should be born in Bethlehem. And the word for 'anointed king' in the Jewish languages, Hebrew and Aramaic, was the word we normally pronounce as '**Messiah**'.

What would the Messiah be like? How would people tell he had arrived? Nobody knew exactly, but there were many theories. Many saw him as a warrior king who would defeat the pagan hordes and establish Israel's freedom. Many saw him as one who would purge the **Temple** and establish true worship. Everybody who believed in such a coming king knew that he would fulfil Israel's scriptures, and bring God's **kingdom** into being at last, on earth as it was in **heaven**. But nobody had a very clear idea of what all this would look like on the ground. In the first century there were several would-be Messiahs who came and went, attracting followers who were quickly dispersed when their leader was caught by the authorities. One thing was certain. To be known as a would-be Messiah was to attract attention from the authorities, and almost certainly hostility.

So when Jesus wanted to put the question to his followers he took them well away from their normal sphere of activity. Caesarea Philippi is in the far north of the land of Israel, well outside the territory of Herod Antipas, a good two days' walk from the sea of Galilee. Even the form of his question, here in Matthew's **gospel** at least, is oblique: 'Who do people say the **son of man** is?', that is, 'Who do people say that this person here, in other words (but without saying it) I myself, am?' Jesus must have known the answer he would get, but he wanted the **disciples** to say it out loud.

The disciples report the general reaction – which tells us a good deal about the way Jesus was perceived by the people at large. Not 'gentle Jesus, meek and mild'; not the cosy, comforting friend of little children; rather, like one of the wild prophets of recent or of ancient times, who had stood up and spoken God's word fearlessly against wicked and rebellious kings. Jesus was acting as a prophet: not simply 'one who foretells the future', but one who was God's mouthpiece against injustice and wickedness in high places.

But within that prophetic ministry there lay hidden another dimension, and Jesus believed – otherwise he would scarcely have asked the question – that his followers had grasped this secret. He was not just God's mouthpiece. He was God's

Messiah. He was not just speaking God's word against the wicked rulers of the time. He was God's king, who would supplant them. That was indeed the conclusion they had reached, and Peter takes on the role of spokesman: 'You are the Messiah,' he says, 'the son of the living God.'

It's important to be clear that at this stage the phrase '**son of God**' did not mean 'the second person of the Trinity'. There was no thought yet that the coming king would himself be divine – though some of the things Jesus was doing and saying must already have made the disciples very puzzled, with a perplexity that would only be resolved when, after his **resurrection**, they came to believe that he had all along been even more intimately associated with Israel's one God than they had ever imagined. No: the phrase 'son of God' was a biblical phrase, indicating that the king stood in a particular relation to God, adopted to be his special representative (see, for instance, 2 Samuel 7.14; Psalm 2.7).

Very soon after Jesus' resurrection, his followers came to believe that the same phrase had a whole other layer of meaning that nobody had hitherto imagined. But it's important, if we are to understand the present passage, that we don't read into it more than is there. What Peter and the others were saying was: you are the true king. You're the one Israel has been waiting for. You are God's adopted son, the one of whom the Psalms and prophets had spoken.

They knew it was risky. With this, they were not only signing on to be part of a prophetic movement that challenged existing authorities in God's name; they were signing on for a royal challenge. Jesus was the true king! That meant that Herod – and even faraway Caesar – had better look out. And as for the Temple authorities . . .

To begin with it looked as though Jesus was simply endorsing their dreams. If Peter had declared that Jesus was the Messiah, Jesus had a word for Peter as well. The name 'Peter', or, in his native Aramaic, 'Cephas', means 'rock' or 'stone'. If Peter was prepared to say that Jesus was the Messiah, Jesus was prepared to say that, with this allegiance, Peter would himself be the foundation for his new building. Just as God gave Abram the name Abraham, indicating that he would be the father of many nations (Genesis 17.5), so now Jesus gives Simon the new name Peter, the Rock.

Furthermore, just as in the Sermon on the Mount Jesus told a story about a wise man building a house on the rock (7.24), so now Jesus himself declares that he's going to do just that. Here, as there, we are meant to imagine in the background the great city, Jerusalem, built on the rocky heights of Mount Zion. In some Jewish traditions, the Temple in Jerusalem was the place where heaven and earth met, and where the gates of the underworld as well were to be found. Jesus is declaring that he is reconstructing this centrepiece of God's world.

Jesus isn't going to build an actual city, or an actual Temple. He is going to build a community, consisting of all those who give allegiance to him as God's anointed king. And this movement, this community, starts then and there, at Caesarea Philippi, with Peter's declaration.

For the moment this must remain deadly secret. If it were to leak out it could be deadly indeed. But to those who agree with Peter that Jesus of Nazareth really is God's Messiah, this promise is made: that, through this allegiance, they will become the people through whom the living God will put the world to rights, bringing heaven and earth into their new state of justice and peace. Peter, with this declaration of **faith**, will be the starting point of this community. Peter has much to learn, and many failures to overcome – including one in the very next passage. But even this is part of the process. Jesus' new community, after all, will consist simply of forgiven sinners.

MATTHEW 16.21–28

Jesus Predicts His Death

²¹From then on Jesus began to explain to his disciples that he would have to go to Jerusalem, and suffer many things from the elders, chief priests and scribes, and be killed, and be raised on the third day.

²²Peter took him and began to tell him off. 'That's the last thing God would want, Master!' he said. 'That's never, ever going to happen to you!'

²³Jesus turned on Peter. 'Get behind me, satan!' he said. 'You're trying to trip me up! You're not looking at things like God does! You're looking at things like a mere mortal!'

²⁴Then Jesus said to his disciples,

'If anyone wants to come after me, they must give themselves up, and pick up their cross, and follow me. ²⁵Yes: if someone wants to save their life, they must lose it; and if anyone loses their life for my sake they will find it. ²⁶What use will it be, otherwise, if you win the whole world but forfeit your true life? What will you give to get your life back? ²⁷You see, the son of man is going to "come in the glory of his father with his angels", and then "he will reward everyone for the work they have done". ²⁸I'm telling you the truth: some of those standing here will not taste death until they see "the son of man coming in his kingdom".'

When Lewis Carroll had become famous through his story *Alice in Wonderland*, he decided to follow it up with a second book in which both he and his readers would need to learn how to think inside out. In *Alice through the Looking Glass* he created a mirror-image world. In order to get somewhere in that world, you discover it's no good trying to walk towards it; you'll look up presently and find you're further away than ever. In order to get there, you must set off in what seems the opposite direction. It takes a sustained mental effort to imagine all the ordinary activities of life working as in a mirror. If you've ever tried to cut your own hair, or trim your own beard, while looking in a mirror, you will know how difficult it is.

What Jesus is now asking of his **disciples** is that they learn to think in a similar inside-out way. To begin with, they find it completely impossible. Peter, speaking for them all, has just told Jesus that as far as they're concerned he is not just a prophet, he's God's anointed king, the **Messiah**. Their natural next move would be to sit down and plan their strategy: if he's the king, and if his people are going to be like the house built on the rock, then they must figure out how to get rid of the present kings and **priests** who are ruling Israel (or, more accurately, misruling it).

The obvious solution would be this: march on Jerusalem, pick up supporters on the way, choose your moment, say your prayers, fight a surprise battle, take over the **Temple**, and install Jesus as king. That's how God's **kingdom** will come! That's how 'the **son of man**' will be exalted in his kingdom! That, we may be sure, was something like what they had in mind.

Jesus' proposal is a through-the-looking-glass version of this. Yes, we'll be going to Jerusalem. Yes, the kingdom of God is coming, coming soon now. Yes, the son of man will be exalted as king, dispensing justice to the world. But the way to this kingdom is by the exact opposite road to the one the disciples – and especially Peter – have in mind. It will involve suffering and death. Jesus will indeed confront the rulers and authorities, the chief priests and **legal experts**, in Jerusalem; but they, not he, will appear to win the battle. He will then be raised from the dead, so Jesus says; but neither Peter nor the others can figure out for the moment what he might mean by this.

All they know is that he is talking nonsense, dangerous nonsense. Not for the last time in the story (see 26.69–75) Peter blunders in with both feet. The 'rock' on whom Jesus said he would build his church turns out, for the moment, to be shifting sand. We can feel the house tottering, ready to fall, before it's even been built. Jesus uses for Peter words he's used before for the arch-enemy, the **satan** itself (4.10). The passage contains a dire warning for all those called to any office or vocation in God's church: the one to whom some of the greatest promises and commissions were made is the one who earned the sharpest rebuke.

Like Paul in his letters, Jesus insists that God thinks differently from how we mortals think. God sees everything inside out; or, perhaps we should say, God sees everything the right way round, whereas we see everything inside out. Paul again: we see at the moment in a puzzling mirror, but eventually we shall see the way God sees (1 Corinthians 13.12).

Once that is clear, the call goes out to follow Jesus, a call which rings down the centuries like a great bell in a distant church, calling us from whatever we're doing. Imagine the bell echoing through the streets of your town: pick up your cross and follow me, pick up your cross and follow me. Imagine its sound resonating through shops and offices, through schoolrooms and hospital wards, through bustling tenements and lonely apartments: pick up your cross and follow me. Imagine people coming out of their doors to see where the noise is coming from, to listen to this great bell; and there, walking ahead of them, is Jesus, a compelling and mysterious figure. Pick up your cross and follow me.

Following him will cost everything and give everything. There are no half measures on this journey. It's going to be like learning to swim: if you keep your foot on the bottom of the pool you'll never work out how to do it. You have to lose your life to find it. What's the use of keeping your feet on the bottom when the water gets too deep? You have the choice: swim or drown. Apparent safety, walking on the bottom, isn't an option any longer.

To those who followed him at the time, Jesus made astonishing claims about what was going to happen in their own lifetime. Many people have been puzzled by these claims, for the simple reason that they have failed to see the significance of what happens at the end of the story. The phrases about 'the son of man coming in his kingdom' and the like are not about what we call the 'second coming' of Jesus. They are about his *vindication*, following his suffering. They are fulfilled when he rises from the dead and is granted 'all authority in **heaven** and on earth' (28.18).

To those who follow him today, Jesus makes equally large promises. He is already the risen and exalted Lord of the world. We don't have to wait, as they did, for his vindication. It's already happened. It remains true that to follow him we have to learn to think inside out, in looking-glass fashion: what the world counts as great is foolishness, and what the world counts folly is the true wisdom. Cling on to your life and you'll lose it; give everything you've got to following Jesus, including life itself, and you'll win it. In every generation there are, it seems, a few people who are prepared to take Jesus seriously, at his word. What would it be like if you were one of them?

MATTHEW 17.1–8

The Transfiguration

¹After six days Jesus took Peter, James, and James's brother John, and led them off up a high mountain by themselves. ²There he was transformed in front of them. His face shone like the sun, and his clothes became as white as light. ³Then, astonishingly, Moses and Elijah appeared to them. They were talking with Jesus.

⁴Peter just had to say something. 'Master,' he said to Jesus, 'it's wonderful for us to be here! If you want, I'll make three shelters here – one for you, one for Moses, and one for Elijah!'

⁵While he was still speaking, a bright cloud overshadowed them. Then there came a voice out of the cloud. 'This is my

dear son,' said the voice, 'and I'm delighted with him. Pay attention to him.'

[6]When the disciples heard this, they fell on their faces and were scared out of their wits. [7]Jesus came up and touched them.

'Get up,' he said, 'and don't be afraid.'

[8]When they raised their eyes, they saw nobody except Jesus, all by himself.

Mount Tabor is a large, round hill in central Galilee. When you go there today with a party of pilgrims, you have to get out of your bus and take a taxi to the top. They say that God is especially pleased with the Mount Tabor taxi-drivers, because more praying goes on in the few minutes hurtling up or down the narrow mountain road in those cars than in the rest of the day, or possibly the week. (I've heard that said of other places, too, but at Mount Tabor it's very believable.)

Mount Tabor is the traditional site of the transfiguration, the extraordinary incident which Matthew, Mark and Luke all relate about Jesus. Actually, we don't know for sure that it took place there. It is just as likely that Jesus would have taken Peter, James and John – his closest associates – up Mount Hermon, which is close to Caesarea Philippi, where the previous conversation took place. Mount Hermon is more remote and inaccessible, which is of course why parties of pilgrims have long favoured Mount Tabor. From both mountains you get a stunning view of Galilee, spread out in front of you.

But Jesus and his three friends weren't looking at the view. They had something much more extraordinary to concentrate on – something so extraordinary, in fact, that many people have found it hard to believe. But the story is so strange – not least Peter's odd blurted-out suggestion about building three shelters! – that many scholars now agree there must have been a real historical event of this kind. And in fact there have been several other recorded instances, both ancient and modern, of similar things happening, when people have been very close to God in joyful prayer.

That reminds us of something important. People often suggest that Jesus was shining brightly because he was divine, and that this was a vision of his divinity, which would otherwise have remained secret. But in Luke's account Moses and Elijah are shining as well, so it can't mean that. Moses and Elijah aren't divine. And in any case Jesus himself had said, earlier in Matthew's **gospel**, that all God's people would shine like stars in God's **kingdom** (13.43, quoting Daniel 12.3). For the New Testament writers in general, in fact, humanity itself is a glorious thing, and Jesus' perfect humanity provides the model for the glory which all his people will one day share. If you want to see Jesus' divinity, the early Christians would tell us, you must look, however surprisingly, at Jesus' suffering and shameful death. If that seems puzzling, it's a puzzle the first Christians insisted we should live with.

In fact, the scene at the transfiguration (as it's normally called) offers a strange parallel and contrast to the crucifixion (Matthew 27.33–54). If you're going to meditate on the one, you might like to hold the other in your mind as well, as a sort of backdrop. Here, on a mountain, is Jesus, revealed in glory; there, on a hill outside Jerusalem, is Jesus, revealed in shame. Here his clothes are shining white; there, they have been stripped off, and soldiers have gambled for them. Here he is flanked by Moses and Elijah, two of Israel's greatest heroes, representing the **law** and the prophets; there, he is flanked by two brigands, representing the level to which Israel had sunk in rebellion against God. Here, a bright cloud overshadows the scene; there, darkness comes upon the land. Here Peter blurts out how wonderful it all is; there, he is hiding in shame after denying he even knows Jesus. Here a voice from God himself declares that this is his wonderful son; there, a pagan soldier declares, in surprise, that this really was God's son.

14

The mountain-top explains the hill-top – and vice versa. Perhaps we only really understand either of them when we see it side by side with the other. Learn to see the glory in the cross; learn to see the cross in the glory; and you will have begun to bring together the laughter and the tears of the God who hides in the cloud, the God who is to be known in the strange person of Jesus himself. This story is, of course, about being surprised by the power, love and beauty of God. But the point of it is that we should learn to recognize that same power, love and beauty within Jesus, and to listen for it in his voice – not least when he tells us to take up the cross and follow him.

Matthew, here as elsewhere, highlights the parallel between Jesus and Moses. Moses led the children of Israel out of Egypt and then, before completing his task, went up Mount Sinai to receive the law. He then went up again, after the Israelites had drastically broken the law, to pray for them and to beg for God's mercy. (Elijah, too, met God in a special way on Mount Sinai; but Matthew's interest, throughout the gospel, is in the way in which Jesus is like Moses, only more so.) Towards the end of Moses' life, God promised to send the people a prophet just like him (Deuteronomy 18), and gave the command: you must listen to him. Now, as Moses once again meets God on the mountain, the voice from the cloud draws attention to Jesus, confirming what Peter had said in the previous chapter. Jesus isn't just a prophet; he is God's own son, the **Messiah**, and God is delighted with what he is doing. The word to the **disciples** then is just as much a word to us today. If you want to find the way – the way to God, the way to the promised land – you must listen to him.

MATTHEW 17.9–13

The Question about Elijah

| [9]As they were coming down the mountain, Jesus gave them |

15

strict instructions. 'Don't tell anyone about the vision,' he said, 'until the son of man has been raised from the dead.'

[10]'So why', asked the disciples, 'do the scribes say that "Elijah must come first"?'

[11]'Elijah does indeed come,' replied Jesus, 'and "he will restore everything". [12]But let me tell you this: Elijah has already come, and they didn't recognize him! They did to him whatever they wanted. That's how the son of man, too, will suffer at their hands.'

[13]Then the disciples realized that he was talking to them about John the Baptist.

The young student nervously approached the professor after the lecture. He'd been thinking for some while about doing graduate work after his degree, and this teacher's lectures were the ones he'd most enjoyed. Could he perhaps have a brief chat?

The professor sat him down in his formidable study. Books lined the walls, papers filled the desk. Feeling very inadequate, the student explained rather lamely what he was interested in, what had excited him about the lectures, and how he'd like some advice about whether it would be good to go on to doctoral work. The professor asked some questions, gave a few suggestions, and then told the student to go to the faculty office and fill in the required form.

The student had heard from friends how these things normally worked. Anxiously he asked if there was supposed to be some kind of official interview, some scrutiny to make sure he was up to the standard.

'We've just had that,' replied the professor, showing him to the door with the hint of a smile.

I know the story is true because, of course, I was the student.

Suddenly the world looked a different place. I was expecting a further stage of the process, and now I discovered I was already past it and through to the world beyond – the world, in my case, of graduate studies, long hours in libraries, and the struggle to write a doctoral dissertation. But that sense of finding yourself a stage further on than you imagined is exactly what the **disciples** found in this curious little conversation with Jesus, immediately after the transfiguration.

'Why do the **scribes** say that Elijah must come first?' What an odd question, we think. Not at all. They had a fixed idea in their heads, like a kind of railway timetable. Here we are, standing on the station platform, waiting for the express to come roaring by on its way to the big city, knowing that our train, the little one that stops at all the smaller stations, will be coming a few minutes afterwards. Then, to our surprise, our train comes first. What's happened? Why does the timetable say that the express should come through ahead?

Ah, says the stationmaster. It was going so fast that you missed it. You turned your back, went for a cup of coffee, and while you were away it came and went. Ah, says Jesus. Elijah is indeed scheduled to appear before the **Messiah**. And it's true! In fact, he's been and gone. You weren't looking in the right place, or in the right way. He has already done his work. And (the implication is) yes, this really is your train. This really is the Messiah.

Where did their railway timetable come from, then? Like almost everything else in Judaism, from their scriptures, the Old Testament. The prophet Malachi declared that God would send Elijah the prophet to prepare the people 'before the great and terrible day of the Lord' (4.5). Elijah had purified the people with terrifying strictness before his own moment of terror, face to face with God on the mountain (1 Kings 19). Eventually, in the story, he was taken up to **heaven** in a whirl-wind. The rumour went round that perhaps he hadn't died properly, that perhaps he would have to return one day.

Malachi makes that hope concrete and specific, and some other later Jewish texts repeat it in various forms. One such text, the Wisdom of Ben Sirach, sometimes called 'Ecclesiasticus'

17

(written about 200 BC), speaks of Elijah 'restoring the tribes of Jacob' (48.10). Jews of the time often referred to their nation in this way; 'Israel' was the special name that God had given to the ancestor Jacob.

Those who studied and taught such texts (the scribes) developed a kind of timetable of events from them. When things got really bad, God would send Elijah to get Israel ready. Then, when the Messiah came, he could take up the work from there.

The disciples are clearly puzzled. They have just declared that Jesus is the Messiah; and now they have seen him conversing with Moses and Elijah. Surely, if he was the Messiah, Elijah should have appeared first, not halfway through his work? Jesus' answer shows that the timetable has moved on without them realizing it. The timetable was correct; but what they had missed was that **John the Baptist** was Elijah. He did his work, and now Jesus is building on it. For neither the first nor the last time, a cryptic reference to John is in fact an even more cryptic reference to Jesus himself (see 11.2–19; 21.23–27).

Why had the disciples not recognized John as Elijah? Because they were looking for the wrong sort of person. It was exactly the same as the reason why they didn't understand Jesus' saying, in the previous chapter and now again here, that he was himself going to suffer and die as the climax of his own vocation.

John the Baptist hadn't come to blast everyone into shape with celestial thunderbolts. He was a voice, warning of what was to come, but himself dying under the weight of the evil he had denounced. Jesus hadn't come to sweep all before him with a blaze of power. He had come to bring God's **kingdom** of love and power, and the way to that kingdom lay down the road of suffering. We shouldn't miss the fact that it was immediately after he had announced his own commitment to that road, and invited his followers to come down it with him, that he was revealed in glory and blazing light on the mountain.

Where are you in God's timetable? Part of the risk of **faith** is that we often don't know the answer to that question in terms of our own personal lives. Often we only discover what God was doing in and through us when we look back. But when we look beyond ourselves to God's wider picture we should know the answer.

The timetable of what God is doing in the world is going ahead. If we want to play our part in it, we must follow where Jesus himself leads: along the way of the cross, of self-renunciation and service. After all, the most important event in the timetable has already occurred. Jesus himself was raised from the dead, the secret is out, and all of history is now bathed in that Easter light. Our task is to find our own role and vocation in following him and helping that light to shine throughout the world.

MATTHEW 17.14–21

Faith that Moves Mountains

¹⁴When they came near the crowd, a man approached and knelt in front of him.

¹⁵'Master,' he said, 'take pity on my son! He suffers from awful fits which are frightful for him. He often falls into the fire, and often into the water. ¹⁶I brought him to your disciples, but they couldn't cure him.'

¹⁷'You unbelieving and twisted generation!' responded Jesus. 'How much longer must I be with you? How much longer must I put up with you? Bring him here to me.'

¹⁸Then Jesus rebuked the demon and it came out of him. The boy was cured from that moment.

¹⁹The disciples came to Jesus in private. 'Why couldn't we cast it out?' they asked.

²⁰'Because of your lack of faith,' Jesus replied. 'I'm telling

you the truth: if you have faith like a grain of mustard seed, you will say to this mountain, "Move from here to there", and it will move. Nothing will be impossible for you. [21]But this kind only comes out by prayer and fasting.'

She was a strong swimmer, and by now she was ready to tackle the challenge of swimming in the sea. A bathing pool is all right to begin with, but it's a bit tame compared with ocean rollers.

For a while it was simply exhilarating. She allowed the giant waves either to carry her off or to break right over her. She adored the feeling of energy as the swell and flow of salt water moved this way and that. She set off from one side of the long, curved bay and swam successfully to the other side, then back again. She could do it! She sat contentedly in the afternoon sunshine, drying off, feeling pleasantly tired, knowing she was up to the challenge of the ocean.

The next day, eager to repeat the experience, she was down on the beach earlier in the day. Again the waves and the swell were dramatic and exciting. But this time, when she set off for the long haul across the mouth of the bay, she felt strangely tired. She didn't seem to be making so much headway. She was battling with the waves, but now, instead of being friendly monsters, they seemed threatening. She began to be nervous, then frightened, then panicky. She felt her strength ebbing away. Finally she shouted for help, once, twice, and again. After what seemed like a thousand hours, in which she became thoroughly cold, frightened and exhausted, the lifeguard's boat arrived. Strong, kind hands helped her out of the water. Moments later she was back on the beach, with a mug of hot coffee, wrapped in a towel, recovering.

'What I don't understand', she said, her teeth chattering with the cold and exhaustion, 'was why it was so easy yesterday and so impossible today.'

'You're not the first person to ask that,' said the lifeguard.

'Some days the tides and currents run differently. It looks the same but there's a huge undertow. One day it's working with you, another day it's against you. That's why you need to be a doubly strong swimmer to come here every day. And actually we get quite cross with people who insist on trying to do it without realizing they're going to need help . . .'

Jesus' **disciples** must have been just as puzzled. Early on in his public career he had commissioned them to do, in pairs but without his own presence, what he had been doing. They were to heal the sick, to raise the dead, to cast out **demons** (10.8) . . . and they'd done it. It must have felt easy to them; deceptively easy, as it turned out. At that stage of Jesus' work, cutting an initial swathe of **kingdom**-announcement through the Galilean countryside, it must have seemed as though nothing could stop them.

And now, with Jesus gone for a day or two up the mountain, they were faced with a new challenge, and they couldn't do anything with it. When Moses came down the mountain, he found that the people, weary with his absence, had already broken the **law** by making a golden calf; and he was naturally very angry. The disciples haven't exactly been rebellious in that sort of way, but Jesus is none the less angry. They should by now have had **faith**! They should have learnt some lessons! A real belief in the real God would have enabled them to deal with this problem as well! After Peter's rebuke, and after looking at their uncomprehending faces when he talked about where his vocation was now taking him, he must have wondered if he was ever going to get the message through to them. Like the swimmer on the second day, they had been faced with a stronger challenge than they had expected, and they hadn't been up to it. Such faith as they possessed had evaporated when they needed it. Maybe they thought they had had the power in themselves; maybe they thought they could do it without bothering God too much . . .

21

The severity of the problem is matched by the astonishing promise that Jesus then makes. It looks as though the boy in question was suffering from something like what we'd call epilepsy. There were and are, however, many different conditions that look similar, and the point is that in this case there was more than simply a proneness to fits. It seemed as though the illness was deliberately destructive, so that instead of the sufferer simply going into convulsions, he was being hurled into fire or water.

Whatever the precise diagnosis, Jesus' comments, after healing the boy, are both encouraging and challenging. If you have faith, he says, even as small as a mustard seed (which, we recall from 13.31–32, is tiny but productive), then nothing will be impossible to you. What he said about the kingdom in the **parable** in chapter 13 he now says about individual faith.

The secret, of course, is that the size of the faith isn't important; what's important is the God in whom you believe. If you want to see the moon, the size of the window you're looking through isn't important; what matters is that it's facing in the right direction. A tiny slit in the wall will do if the moon is that side of the house. A huge window facing in the wrong direction will be no good at all. That's what true faith is like. The smallest prayer to the one true God will produce great things; the most elaborate devotions to a 'god' of your own making, or indeed someone else's, will be useless, or worse.

Jesus knows from the disciples' failure that they are still not in tune with the true God who is calling them, as well as him, to obedience and to the way of the cross. In the last verse of the passage (which some of the best Greek manuscripts miss out; that's why some of the English versions don't have it) he challenges them, and us, to a further exercise of faith. Once you are looking at the moon through the right window, maybe you should get out your telescope and study it in more detail. Once you are getting to know the one true God, maybe it's

22

time for some more concentrated prayer, perhaps even with the discipline of fasting to concentrate your mind and heart. If Jesus himself needed these disciplines, who are we to think we can manage without them?

MATTHEW 17.22–27

The Temple Tax

²²As they regathered in Galilee, Jesus said to them, 'The son of man is going to be given over into the hands of sinners. ²³They will kill him, and on the third day he will be raised.' And they were very sad.

²⁴They came to Capernaum, where the officials who collected the Temple tax approached Peter.

'Your teacher pays the Temple tax, doesn't he?' they asked.

²⁵'Yes,' he replied.

When he came into the house, Jesus said to him, 'What d'you think, Simon? When the kings of the world collect taxes or duties, who do they collect them from? From their own families, or from outsiders?'

²⁶'From outsiders,' he replied.

'Well then,' said Jesus, 'that means the families are free. ²⁷But we don't want to give them offence, do we? So why don't you go down to the sea and cast out a hook? The first fish you catch, open its mouth and you'll find a coin. Take that and give it to them for the two of us.'

Jesus told them they were going to be fishers of men, not of money (4.19)! This is one of the most peculiar little stories in the whole New Testament. What on earth does it mean?

One day the bishop parked his car, as usual, outside his house. He knew that the City Council had just passed a by-law requiring everybody to pay for parking spaces in that street. He knew they had done it because they wanted to make life difficult for the church. But he parked there anyway.

Sure enough, within minutes a parking attendant rang the doorbell. The bishop's chaplain answered it.

'You do know you've got to pay to park here?' said the attendant.

The chaplain came indoors to the bishop. The bishop knew that sooner or later he would have to take a stand, to make the point that the church was there to serve the city and that the charge was unjust. But this wasn't the moment. No sense in wasting time and energy protesting to a minor official.

'I tell you what, John,' said the bishop. 'The garbage truck is coming down the road. When it stops, reach inside the back and you'll find an old cigarette packet. Inside it you'll find a coin. Give that to the attendant. That'll keep her happy.'

No, it's not an exact parallel, but it catches something of the flavour of the story. Jesus didn't believe the **Temple** tax was proper. Every Jew, all over the world, was supposed to pay a small sum each year (a 'didrachma', a little coin), to help to support the Temple in Jerusalem. This was, we may suppose, one of many minor irritants that caused several Jews of the time to dislike the Temple regime and want to overthrow it. And it may have been a small part of what Jesus himself had against the Temple. It was the house built on sand, and it would be overthrown (7.26–27). It was where the gates of the underworld were to be found, that would oppose the new 'building' he was constructing (16.18). Beautiful and holy as it was, it had become a den of brigands (21.13), and God's judgment was hanging over it by a slender thread (24.2).

But now was not the time, Galilee was not the place, and a minor tax-collector was not the person, for Jesus' major protest to be made. Before too long he would be in the Temple itself, turning over tables, spilling coins to right and left (21.12). For the moment it was better not to raise the alarm, not to let word get out that his **kingdom**-movement was indeed aimed at challenging the authority of the Temple and its rulers. So the tax had better be paid.

But how to do it? One of the interesting things about the way Matthew has told this story (none of the other **gospels** have it) is that he doesn't say, as he might well have done, 'So Peter went off and caught a fish and found the coin as Jesus had said.' We are left to speculate whether he really did, or whether this was some kind of private joke, a way of telling Peter to catch a fish and sell it to pay the tax.

Whatever we think about that, the tone of the whole story implies that for Jesus this was a way of making light of the whole system, maybe even making fun of it. 'Oh, they want Temple money, do they? Well, why don't you go fishing . . . I'm sure you'll find something good enough for them.' It was a way of *not* saying, on the one hand, 'Oh yes, of course, we'll certainly pay – here, take a coin from my purse!', or, on the other hand, 'No, certainly not, the whole system is corrupt – go and give him a punch on the nose!' It was a way of biding time.

It corresponds, in other words, to the way Jesus told strange **parables** and didn't usually explain them to the crowds. The time would come when he would speak more openly, more directly, more threateningly . . . yes, precisely when he was in Jerusalem, turning over tables and driving out traders. This story looks forward to that moment, but it also says that the moment isn't here yet.

The point of the story, then, isn't that Jesus had the power to make a coin appear in the mouth of a fish – though that is certainly implied. Nor is it that Jesus is simply a good citizen, finding ways of paying the necessary taxes. The point is that he was a master strategist. He was himself, as he told his **disciples** to be, as wise as a serpent while remaining as innocent as a dove (10.16). There is, perhaps, a model there for all his followers as they pray and wait and plan how to confront the powers of this world with the subversive **message** of the kingdom of God.

MATTHEW 18.1–7
Humility and Danger

[1]At that time the disciples came to Jesus.

'So, then,' they said, 'who is the greatest in the kingdom of heaven?'

[2]Jesus called a child and stood her in the middle of them.

[3]'I'm telling you the truth,' he said. 'Unless you turn inside out and become like children, you will never, ever, get into the kingdom of heaven. [4]So if any of you make yourselves humble like this child, you will be great in the kingdom of heaven. [5]And if anyone welcomes one such child in my name, they welcome me.'

[6]'Whoever causes one of these little ones who believe in me to trip up,' he went on, 'it would be better for them to have a huge millstone hung around their neck and be drowned far out in the deep sea. [7]It's a terrible thing for the world that people will be made to stumble. Obstacles are bound to appear and trip people up, but it will be terrible for the person who makes them come.'

Among the saddest sights in our world, some of the worst, I think, are the glimpses we get of children in need.

I think of three children grubbing around in a stinking, smouldering garbage heap on the edge of a South American city. They are barely old enough to go to school, but they are already streetwise. They know what to look for, things which they can sell for a few small coins to get a little food and drink. Their young faces tell the story of the adult world where, despite their years, they are now at home.

I think of a whole school in Uganda where almost every child is an orphan because of the AIDS epidemic. For the

26

same reason, every single teacher has a class of over a hundred children.

I think, too, of the rich and spoilt children growing up in the Western world, needing more electronic toys and gadgets to keep them amused because nobody has introduced them to books and music and country walks.

What we do with our children – and what we do *to* them – is a worryingly accurate indication of what we think about the world, God and ourselves. To many adults, children are just a nuisance. But the point is that they're a nuisance (if they are) because they matter. They disturb our organized adult world because they are real people. If they were toys or machines we could put them away in a cupboard. But we can't. They have their own dignity, their own questions, their own future, their own unique identity.

Many societies have done their best to ignore this, and in the ancient world it was often forgotten altogether. Children were frequently seen as only half-human until they had reached puberty, perhaps for the worrying reason that until they were available as sexual partners adults wouldn't want to know about them. Girls in particular suffered. Often newborn girls were simply thrown away – left to starve or be eaten by predators, or sold for prostitution at an early age – because the family didn't want another expensive daughter to bring up. It is significant that in some languages, including the Greek in which the New Testament is written, the words for 'child' are mostly neither masculine nor feminine, but neuter: the child wasn't a 'he' or a 'she', but simply an 'it'.

The child in this story is an 'it' in Greek (verse 2). But I have guessed, in the translation, that 'it' was a girl, not least because a girl would make with special clarity the point Jesus was wanting to get into the **disciples**' minds: that the weakest, most vulnerable, least significant human being you can think of is the clearest possible signpost to what the **kingdom of God** will be like. God's kingdom – the future time when '**heaven**' rules on earth – won't be about the survival of the fittest. It won't be the result of some long evolutionary process in which the strongest, the fastest, the loudest, the angriest people get to the front ahead of everyone else.

When the disciples asked who was to be the greatest in the heavenly rule that was to come on earth, we are probably right to suspect that it was things like this they had in mind. They knew about the heroes of old. They had lists of them. Along with **faith** and hope, military courage and success tend to loom large among their qualities. Jesus tosses all that out of the window, and instead calls out a little child: shy, vulnerable, unsure of herself, but trusting and with clear eyes, ready to listen, to be loved and to love, to learn and grow. This is what true greatness is like, he says. Go and learn about it.

In particular, go and imitate it. That means, as he says, being turned inside out or back to front. It means learning to look at life, at the world, at God, at yourself, through the other end of the telescope. We all find it difficult (particularly a group of youngish men like the disciples) to think that weakness and vulnerability are anything other than things to be ashamed of. But humility is what counts in God's kingdom, because pride and arrogance are the things which, more than anything else in God's world, distort and ultimately destroy human lives – their own, and those of people they affect.

But, here and in the next passage, Jesus is concerned not just with helping his followers to learn this lesson. He doesn't just want them to see that becoming like children was central to their growing in grace and wisdom, in kingdom-greatness. He is, of course, concerned for children themselves. He doesn't have a romantic, cosy vision in which children can just play happily. Precisely because they are so trusting, so eager, they are of all people the most at risk. This remains as true today as ever it was.

So Jesus issues a stark warning, with typical exaggeration. There must be easier ways of drowning someone than making them carry an enormous millstone around their neck and taking them in a boat far out to sea so that they can sink into the deepest part; but that's what his picture suggests, like a vivid and overdramatized cartoon. Large circular stones, with a central hole for the mechanism, were used to grind corn; the biggest were so large it took a donkey to work them. That's the type Jesus is talking about, the type he says you should imagine having round your neck as a collar. And he doesn't just talk of people being 'thrown into the sea'; he is talking of the deep sea, far out, away from the shore.

If this seems violent or extreme, perhaps it's because we, too, have undervalued the 'little ones' Jesus is talking about – children in particular, of course, but also all those who are powerless, vulnerable, at risk in our world. Exploitation of such people is inevitable, granted the way the world now is. But those who indulge in it are given this warning, far sterner than anything that Jesus ever says about what we think of as the 'big' sins such as murder, adultery and theft. They matter, but causing one of the little ones to 'stumble' or 'trip up' matters even more. Harsh words to address a harsh reality. Learning about God's kingdom means facing the real evils of the world and realizing that God hates them far more than we do.

MATTHEW 18.8–14

More about the 'Little Ones'

[8]'But if your hand or your foot causes you to trip up,' Jesus continued, 'cut it off and throw it away. It's better to enter into life crippled or lame than to go into eternal fire with both hands and both feet! [9]And if your eye causes you to trip up, pull it out and throw it away. Life with one eye is better than hell with two!

¹⁰'Take care not to despise one of these little ones. I tell you this: in heaven, their angels are always gazing on the face of my father who lives there.

¹²'How does it seem to you? If someone has a hundred sheep and one of them wanders off and goes missing, what will he do? He'll leave the ninety-nine on the hillside and go off after the one that's missing, won't he? ¹³And when, eventually, he finds it, I'll tell you the truth: he will celebrate over that one more than over the ninety-nine who didn't go missing! ¹⁴It's the same with your father in heaven. The last thing he wants is for a single one of these little ones to be lost.'

Our neighbour was walking by the beach one day, with her dog, when suddenly the dog stopped and sniffed, and looked puzzled and wary. She stopped too, but she couldn't see anything. Then she looked hard at the rocks in front of the dog, just above the line of the tide.

And then she saw it. It was a baby seal, camouflaged against the colour of rocks and sea, washed up and unable to get away. It was far more frightened of the dog and the human than the dog was of it. Its reaction was interesting, indeed charming. It had put up its flippers in a half-successful attempt to cover its face. That's not what a seal's flippers were meant for, but it was the best it could do. If it covered its face, it seemed to think, it would be in less danger.

When I heard this story my mind went straight (as you might expect a theologian's mind to do) to the Bible, to the wonderful picture in Isaiah 6, where the living God, the terrifying Holy One of Israel, appears to Isaiah in the **Temple** in order to commission him as a prophet. The prophet sees God directly, and imagines this will mean his death. As everyone knew, nobody gets to see God and live. But he also sees the angels, the 'seraphim', who are God's attendants in the heavenly throne-room. They are flying around him, for which they need, as you might suppose, two wings each. But they have six wings each, not two. With two of the spare, non-flying wings they are covering their feet, for reasons that are now obscure to us. But with the other two wings they are doing what the baby seal was doing on the beach. They are covering their faces, hiding them in awe before the glory, beauty and majesty of the living God.

That is, in fact, the normal condition of angels in Jewish pictures of the heavenly realm or courtroom. Many Christians today tend to forget how awesome the living God is, but the ancient Jews seldom forgot, and the angels they spoke of – surrounding God's throne, waiting on him, flying at once to do his bidding – almost always covered their faces to avoid looking directly at God.

And this is the point: *the angels who look after these 'little ones' don't have to cover their faces*. They are allowed, welcomed even, to look on God directly. That's how important they are – or rather, that's how important these 'little ones' are to God.

So who are these 'little ones'? They include weak, vulnerable children, of course, as we were thinking in the previous passage. But they also include those who are weak and vulnerable at other times of life, too: the cripples, the chronically sick, the elderly and infirm, refugees, women (in many cultures), any who find themselves on the human scrap-heap that our world throws people on to when it can't think what else to do with them.

They include the dirty begger you avoided in the street yesterday. They include the shop-girl who you were tempted to be rude to (or to be rude about behind her back). They include the old woman pushing a supermarket trolley down the street with (so it seemed) all her life's belongings piled high on it. They include the teenage boy who drifted into drugs because there weren't any jobs, and who is now dying of heroin.

It's interesting that our modern culture tends, as we say, to 'screen out' people like that. *We* hide our faces from *them*, in a strange parody of the fact that their guardian angels are among the few who don't have to hide their faces from *God*. We are ashamed of them; God isn't. We don't want to know about them; God wants to let them into his closest, most intimate presence. We regard them as undesirable; God desires not only their welfare but their company. They are a standing reminder of God's **kingdom**, and we turn away from them as a society because as a society we have turned away from God.

The other picture is better known, but still striking. The shepherd leaving the ninety-nine sheep while he goes looking for the lost one is the subject of pictures and songs in many Christian traditions. But the point is the same. The sovereign God isn't happy to say 'well, we've still got ninety-nine, let's not worry about the odd silly one that drifts away from the flock – probably not worth much anyway.' No: this is the one that matters.

Put that together with the worrying warnings of verses 8–9, and what do we get? Of course, we know that Jesus didn't mean us literally to cut off hands and feet and pluck out eyes. That kind of self-mutilation is a sign of mental disorder, not of genuine holiness. It's like the two-ton millstone round the neck: a huge exaggeration to make the point.

But the point is no less serious for that. Anyone who has ever tried to break a bad moral habit will know that it some-times feels like cutting off a hand or foot. Anyone who tries to stop a bad attitude towards others will know that it's almost as hard as plucking out an eye. And the habits and attitudes that Jesus has in his sights in this passage are as hard as any. Cutting off the 'hand' that refuses to give to the poor; cutting off the 'foot' that refuses to walk to the soup kitchen to help out; and, in particular, plucking out the 'eye' that refuses to notice the weak, the vulnerable, the helpless all around us, in our cities, on our streets, in our wider world: all these pose a challenge every bit as severe today as the day Jesus first issued it.

MATTHEW 18.15–20

Reconciliation and Prayer in the Community

[15]'If another disciple sins against you,' Jesus continued, 'go and have it out, just between the two of you alone. If they listen to you, you've won back a brother or sister. [16]But if they won't listen, you should take with you one or two others, so that "everything may be established from the mouth of two or three witnesses". [17]If they won't listen to them, tell it to the assembly. And if they won't listen to the assembly, you should treat such a person like you would a Gentile or a tax-collector. [18]I'm telling you the truth: whatever you tie up on earth will be tied up in heaven; and whatever you untie on earth will be untied in heaven.

[19]'Again, let me tell you the truth: if two of you come to an agreement on earth about any matter that you want to ask, it will be done for you by my father in heaven. [20]Yes: where two or three come together in my name, I'll be there in the midst of them.'

Soap operas are a signpost of modern culture. They divide us into two types: some love them, others hate them. Many are addicted to them, know the characters inside out, read magazines about them, write them letters (even though they know they're not real people!), and discuss with their own family and friends what they should or shouldn't do next. Equally, lots of people find the programmes appalling, and would rather stare at a blank television screen than watch five minutes of them.

I confess that I have often been in the second category. (I hope that won't make half my readers throw the book away. This passage, after all, is about reconciliation between people with different points of view!) But recently I've noticed something in the soap operas that some of my family watch. They often include scenes of conflict: painful disagreements between parents and children, teenage brothers or sisters, young adults with different viewpoints.

And sometimes they really do offer role models for how to engage in conflict and disagreement with clarity and honesty. Sometimes they really do get to the bottom of an issue, showing how to put the problem fair and square on the table, how to express anger, confusion and hurt while trying to see the other point of view as well.

Actually, I think reconciliation – real reconciliation, not patched-up splits that will open again under pressure – happens more often in soap operas than in real life. That's fine. We all need lessons in how to do it. If people watch fictional characters working through difficult issues, there's a chance they will start to do it for themselves.

It's time in today's culture that we took reconciliation seriously, and this passage in Matthew 18 is bedrock for the basic principles. Whenever I have been involved in difficult discussions within a family or a Christian fellowship, this is the passage I've always tried to bear in mind. It is severely practical as well as ruthlessly idealistic: not a bad combination.

Reconciliation is a huge issue today. We see clearly the results of *not* doing it: suicide bombs, campaigns of terror, heavy-handed repression by occupying forces. That's on the large scale. On the smaller scale, we see broken marriages, shattered families, feuds between neighbours, divided churches.

Many of us prefer to pretend there isn't a problem. We can refuse to face the facts, swallow our anger or resentment, paper over the cracks, and carry on as if everything is normal while seething with rage inside. Or we can simply avoid and ignore the other person or group, and pretend they don't exist. That may sometimes be the only way (when a total stranger offends you, for instance, and you don't have a chance to talk to them and work it through). But usually it's disastrous.

Many Christians have taken the paper-over-the-cracks option, believing that this is what 'forgiveness' means – pretending that everything is all right, that the other person hasn't really done anything wrong. That simply won't do. If someone else – another Christian in particular! – has been offensive, aggressive, bullying, dishonest, or immoral, nothing whatever is gained by trying to create 'reconciliation' without confronting the real evil that's been done. Forgiveness doesn't mean saying 'it didn't really happen' or 'it didn't really matter'. In either of those cases, you don't need forgiveness, you just need to clear up a misunderstanding. Forgiveness is when it *did* happen, and it *did* matter, and you're going to deal with it and end up loving and accepting one another again anyway. That's why the sequence recommended here is vital.

First go and see the person, one on one. That needs courage; it also needs prayer and humility. The other person may well respond with a counter-accusation, and there may be truth in it which you need to recognize – though it certainly isn't always the case that both sides are equally to blame.

If that works – and I have known the joy of it on more than one occasion, sometimes when I've been rightly accused of something and sometimes when I've had to confront someone else – then it's wonderful. 'You've gained a brother or sister,' says Jesus, and that really is what it feels like. Reconciliation often creates a closer bond than you had in the first place.

But if it doesn't work, and if after thought and prayer you are still convinced there is a wrong to be settled, take one or two others with you. This, of course, is a reality check on your own judgment; you should choose people who are prepared to tell you some uncomfortable truths if that's what's needed. And, if you are in the right but the person refuses to see it, they are your witnesses that you're not just making it up (the quotation about needing 'two or three' comes from the Old Testament law about evidence).

The final act is to inform the local Christian assembly. The word for 'assembly' is the word that later gets translated 'church', but in Jesus' day, and for some while afterwards, Jesus' followers continued to meet in their local synagogues, for which the same word could be used. But Jesus himself probably envisaged little groups or cells of his followers meeting together, praying the special prayer he gave them, reminding one another of his teaching and trying to live it out (particularly his emphasis on forgiveness and remission of debt), and acting as small-scale, localized assemblies of God's renewed people. That would then be the group that should be told about any confrontation that had remained unresolved.

Now comes the hardest part. If someone still refuses to yield and be reconciled, they must be treated as an outcast. (Paul wrestles with the same problem in 1 Corinthians 5.) We don't like the sound of this, but we need to ask what the alternatives are. If there is real evil involved, refusal to face it means a necessary break of fellowship. Reconciliation can only come *after* the problem has been faced.

Together with this hard and high challenge, there go dramatic promises. We aren't left on our own as we struggle to become the sort of communities, families and churches that Jesus is describing. God's presence is with us; our actions on earth have an extra, hidden dimension, the heavenly counterpart of what we do here. And, when we pray together in Christian fellowship, we are therefore assured of being heard and answered. Because, in a promise that remains central to everything that Christians ever do together, 'where two or three' (or two hundred or three hundred, for that matter, but it's often the small groups that need this encouragement most) 'gather in Jesus' name, he is there in the midst of them'. That's not just a promise that we will sense his presence. It's a promise – and a warning! – that he will see and know the innermost truth of everyone's heart. If we take that seriously, engaging in reconciliation will still be costly. But it will always be done in real hope, with joy waiting round the corner for those who persevere.

MATTHEW 18.21–35

The Challenge of Forgiveness

[21]Then Peter came to Jesus.

'Master,' he said, 'how many times must I forgive my brother when he sins against me? As many as seven times?'

[22]'I wouldn't say seven times,' replied Jesus. 'Why not – seventy times seven?'

[23]'So, you see,' he went on, 'the kingdom of heaven is like a royal personage who wanted to settle up accounts with his servants. [24]As he was beginning to sort it all out, one man was brought before him who owed ten thousand talents. [25]He had no means of paying it back, so the master ordered him to be sold, with his wife and children and everything he possessed, and payment to be made.

[26]'So the servant fell down and prostrated himself before the master.

'"Have mercy on me," he said, "and I'll pay you everything!"

[27]'The master was very sorry for the servant, and let him off. He forgave him the loan.

[28]'But that servant went out and found one of his fellow-servants, who owed him a hundred dinars. He seized him and began to throttle him. "Pay me back what you owe me!" he said.

[29]'The colleague fell down and begged him, "Have mercy on me, and I'll pay you!"

[30]'But he refused, and went and threw him into prison until he could pay the debt.

[31]'So when his fellow-servants saw what had happened, they were very upset. They went and informed their master about the whole affair. [32]Then his master summoned him.

'"You're a scoundrel of a servant!" he said to him. "I let you off the whole debt, because you begged me to. [33]Shouldn't you have taken pity on your colleague, like I took pity on you?"

[34]'His master was angry, and handed him over to the torturers, until he had paid the whole debt. [35]And that's what my heavenly father will do to you, unless each of you forgives your brother or sister from your heart.'

Many years ago I was working in a student community. I sometimes assisted in leading worship or preaching for one particular group of students. They were theological students, training for ministry, but shared their accommodation with others from a wide range of subjects – and with a wide range of ideals and standards. I had agreed, some while before, to preach at a midweek service in which the assigned reading, as I knew long in advance, was the passage we're now looking at. What none of us knew was that it was going to be frighteningly relevant.

That week there was a near-riot. Some of the other students living in the residence had been behaving very disruptively. They were making it almost impossible for their colleagues to sleep at night, to study during the day, or to have any peace and quiet. Most of the students didn't even like to invite friends round because the place was so unpleasant. A difficult atmosphere developed as some of the Christian students simply wanted to 'forgive' the troublemakers, in other words not to deal with the problem, while others wanted to make an angry protest, to demand their rights to live in peace and to insist that the disruptive students were dismissed or at least suspended.

So on that weekday lunchtime, at our regular service, you could have heard a pin drop when we heard Matthew 18.21–35 – the passage now in front of you – as the main reading. And my heart was thumping as I stood up to preach about it.

It's a long time ago, and sadly I can't find the notes of what I said. But the lesson of the story is so massive and obvious that I don't really need to look it up. There are several ways of putting the point. Every time you accuse someone else, you accuse yourself. Every time you forgive someone else, though, you pass on a drop of water out of the bucketful that God has already given you. From God's point of view, the distance between being ordinarily sinful (what we all are) and extremely sinful (what the people we don't like seem to be) is like the distance between London and Paris seen from the point of view of the sun. And so on. We can all relate to that.

The key thing, as I have already said, is not that one should therefore swallow all resentment and 'forgive and forget' as though nothing had happened. The key thing is that one should never, ever give up making forgiveness and reconciliation one's goal. If confrontation has to happen, as it often does, it must always be with forgiveness in mind, never revenge.

But underneath that there is another lesson, more subtle perhaps but equally important. Why does Jesus solemnly say, in the last verse, that those who refuse to forgive will themselves be refused forgiveness? Isn't that, to put it bluntly, so harsh as to be out of keeping with the rest of the **gospel**? Can't God override our failings at exactly that point?

Apparently not. At least, I don't know about 'can't', but it seems that he won't. The New Testament speaks with one voice on this subject. Forgiveness isn't like a Christmas present that a kindly grandfather can go ahead and give to a sulky grandchild even if the grandchild hasn't bought a single gift for anyone else. It isn't like the meal that will be waiting for you back home even if you failed to buy a cheese sandwich and a cup of tea for a tramp on the street. It's a different sort of thing altogether.

Forgiveness is more like the air in your lungs. There's only room for you to inhale the next lungful when you've just breathed out the previous one. If you insist on withholding it, refusing to give someone else the kiss of life they may desperately need, you won't be able to take any more in yourself, and you will suffocate very quickly. Whatever the spiritual, moral and emotional equivalent of the lungs may be (we sometimes say 'the heart', but that of course is a metaphor as well), it's either open or closed. If it's open, able and willing to forgive others, it will also be open to receive God's love and forgiveness. But if it's locked up to the one, it will be locked up to the other.

This is a hard lesson to learn, in our thinking and also in our acting. It goes back, like everything else in Matthew 18, to the picture of the child. What is it that stops us either saying 'sorry' or saying 'I forgive you'? Isn't it just that unchildishness, that I'm-too-important-to-do-that-ness, which shows that we have forgotten, or never perhaps learned, that the greatest in the **kingdom of heaven** is the one who has been turned inside out and has become like a little child?

This chapter forms the fourth of Matthew's great collections of Jesus' sayings (after 5—7, 10 and 13); there is one more to go (23—25). It is every bit as challenging as the rest. Its central and sharpest point is just this: that Jesus is establishing God's 'new **covenant**' with Israel and the world. As the prophet Jeremiah saw half a millennium earlier (Jeremiah 31.34), the way of life which will mark out that new covenant is forgiveness. Jesus has already taught his followers to pray for it (6.12), and has specified clearly that if you want forgiveness you've got to be prepared to give it (6.14–15). Now he returns to the theme.

Peter's question and Jesus' answer say it all (verses 21–22). If you're still counting how many times you've forgiven someone, you're not really forgiving them at all, but simply postponing revenge. 'Seventy times seven' is a typical bit of Jesus' teasing. What he means, of course, is 'don't even think about counting; just do it'.

MATTHEW 19.1–9

The Question about Divorce

[1]So this is what happened next. When Jesus had finished saying all this, he went away from Galilee and came to the region of Judaea around the Jordan. [2]Large crowds followed him, and he healed them there.

[3]Some Pharisees approached him with a trick question.

'Is it lawful', they asked, 'for a man to divorce his wife for any reason at all?'

[4]'Haven't you read', he replied, 'that the creator from the beginning "made them male and female"? [5]And this is what he said: "For this reason a man shall leave his father and mother and be joined to his wife, and the two shall become one flesh"? [6]As a result, they are no longer two, but one flesh. So humans shouldn't split up what God has joined together.'

[7]'So then,' they asked, 'why did Moses command that one should give the woman a certificate of divorce and make the separation legal?'

[8]'Moses gave you this command about how to divorce your wives,' replied Jesus, 'because your hearts were hard. But that's not how it was at the beginning. [9]Let me tell you this: anyone who divorces his wife, except for immorality, and marries another woman, commits adultery.'

Last time we bought a car I was startled to notice, in the book of instructions, a list of things to do if you were involved in an accident. Call the police. Make a note of exactly what happened, where and how. Write down the registration numbers of other cars involved. And so on. There was also a section on how to cope if the car began to skid, or did other dangerous things.

Such a section is surprising because you don't really expect the manufacturers of a car to want you to have an accident, to skid, to drive dangerously. (I suppose they might sell more cars if we went round smashing them up all the time, but I don't think that's the point.) And of course they don't. They want you to drive safely, free of trouble, anxiety and danger. But sometimes people do get into difficult situations, and it's important to know what to do if the occasion arises. It would be absurd to suggest that the people who wrote the instruction book were either hoping for such things to happen or even encouraging people to make them happen.

The **Pharisees** seem to have thought that the very existence of legislation about divorce, within the **law** of Moses, meant that Moses was quite happy for it to take place. Since there's a law which tells you how to do it, they seem to have reasoned, that must mean it's all right. Jesus shows the flaw in their thinking by pointing them back to the original intention. Just as a car is made to drive safely on the road, not to skid around colliding with other cars, so marriage was made to be a partnership of one woman and one man for life, not something that could be split up and reassembled whenever one person wanted it (often, in that world and in ours, this would be the man, though this would not always be the case). Moses didn't say, as it were, 'when you drive your car, this is how to have an accident'; rather, 'when you drive a car, take care not to have an accident; but if, tragically, an accident occurs, this is how to deal with it'.

Jesus is quite clear, then, that the Bible does not encourage divorce – just as we would be quite clear that the car manual is not encouraging dangerous driving. But he goes a stage further as well. He is claiming that with his own work God's whole plan has shifted a stage forwards. He is, so to speak, designing cars that shouldn't have accidents. Dangerous driving need no longer happen. He is moving the story of God and his people into a new mode, where the law of Moses won't be the only thing that guides them. God is now in the business of making people new from the inside.

This is almost equally startling, and it often seems a claim that we can't justify. Jesus says that Moses gave the commandments he did because Israel's hearts were hard. Here and elsewhere in the New Testament we find an analysis like this: the Old Testament, though it was indeed the *word* of God, was the word of God for people in the days prior to the new *work* of God that would happen in and through Jesus himself. And, here and elsewhere (e.g. 15.15–20), Jesus seems to be claiming that, through this work, the root problem of the human race, the wickedness of the heart, will itself be dealt with. If that's happening, it ought to function like an automatic steering and power device on a car, that will prevent skids and accidents before they even start to happen.

Ah, but that's the problem. It's not automatic. Just because you sign on as a follower of Jesus, that doesn't mean you won't be tempted to do many wrong things. In fact, it means that temptation levels will almost certainly increase. It will be like driving against the stream of traffic, and sometimes it will seem as though accidents are almost inevitable. But that's precisely because, when God rescues your heart from its natural rebellion, and makes it new through your trust in him, your **baptism** and your following of Jesus, the way this newness works must be *through* your own decisions, your own thinking things through, your own will-power (aided and strengthened at every point, Christians would say, by the **holy spirit**, Jesus' own spirit).

God wants real people, not puppets. The renewal of life he offers, in the sphere of marriage as everywhere else, will come through the willing, intelligent obedience of wholehearted women and men who think out what it means to be loyal to God and to other people, especially to their marriage partner, and who take steps to put it into practice.

In Matthew's **gospel**, uniquely, the very black-and-white teaching on divorce as it appears in Mark and Luke (that divorce shouldn't happen among Jesus' followers) is nuanced.

If one partner has been sexually unfaithful, that may consti-tute grounds for divorce; and divorce will imply a freedom to marry again. In 1 Corinthians 7.15 Paul allows a further ground: if an unbelieving partner desires to separate from a Christian believer, the believer should not ultimately refuse. But in both cases it is quite clear that the Christian norm is lifelong marriage.

Marriage is, after all, one of the principal ways in which the image of the one true God is reflected into the world. The passage Jesus quotes in verse 4 from Genesis 1.27 ('male and female he created them') is the same passage in which it says that we are made in God's image. No wonder it's a hard, costly and wonderful thing to work at a marriage and truly to become 'one flesh'. Jesus' whole aim was to bring about that renewal of the world in which the intention of the creator God would at last be fulfilled. No wonder he didn't want us to settle for anything less than the best.

MATTHEW 19.10–15
Marriage, Celibacy and Children

[10]The disciples said to Jesus, 'If that's the situation of a man with his wife, it would be better not to marry!'

[11]'Not everyone can accept this word,' replied Jesus; 'only the people it's given to. [12]You see, there are some eunuchs who are that way from birth. There are some who have been made eunuchs by others. And there are some who have made themselves eunuchs for the sake of the kingdom of heaven. If anyone can receive this, let them do so.'

[13]Then children were brought to Jesus for him to lay his hands on them and pray. The disciples spoke sternly to them. [14]But Jesus said, 'Let the children come to me! Don't stop them! They are the sort the kingdom of heaven belongs to!' [15]And he laid his hands on them.

Then he moved on elsewhere.

We were staying with friends who had recently become grandparents for the first time. They were telling us of the time when their little granddaughter came to stay overnight while her parents were away for a short while.

'We were so nervous,' they said. 'We wanted to do everything right. If she so much as stirred in her sleep, we jumped up to check she was all right. And when she was crawling around during the day, we had to keep moving things out of her way, and making sure she didn't grab something that might hurt her. We were on watch the whole time! It was exhausting!'

'So you're not going to do that again in a hurry?' I asked, knowing the answer I would get.

'Absolutely! As soon as they'll let us! We adored having her! Next week, we hope!' they responded. The joy of a little child bringing new life into the house far outweighed, for them, the strain and worry of having to look after her.

But by no means all adults, in all societies, have taken the same view. Many have tried to push children into a corner, literally or metaphorically, where they couldn't disrupt the neat and tidy universe that adults have created for themselves. 'Little boys', it used to be said where I came from, 'should be seen and not heard.' All that's changed, of course, but there are still many adults, and adult organizations, and adult ways of life, that squeeze children out, try to ignore them, regard them as a nuisance, and pretend that 'real' life is only for those over a certain age.

Jesus cuts straight through all that. He isn't bothered by the fact that some of the children who are brought to him can't talk properly, that some may be dirty and smelly, and that some will be up to mischief the moment they think nobody's looking. He simply relishes the young life, bubbling up like water from a fountain and refusing to be quenched. That's what God's **kingdom** is like – full of new and unpredictable life. Little children, trusting, adventurous, eager, ready to be drawn into stories and dramas, are just the sort of people the kingdom is for. As in chapter 9, this is a rebuke to the **disciples**: if they are trying to stop children coming to Jesus, this shows that they've got their priorities exactly upside down.

It is significant that the little scene with the children is placed right after the discussion about whether or not to marry. The disciples are startled at Jesus' very rigorous teaching about divorce. They are contemplating the possibility (too late for some of them!) that maybe it would be better not to risk marriage if one was going to be locked into it for life. Some today might respond in the same way – though with the intention of then drawing the conclusion that Jesus' teaching is hopelessly unrealistic.

In response, Jesus says some mysterious words about those who don't marry, either because they decide not to or because they can't. In his culture, most people were married at what, to the modern West, seems quite an early age. Girls in particular were often married soon after puberty. Where life expectancy was low, it was important to make full use of childbearing years. Many young men would be married well before the age of 20.

But there were always some who were physically incapable of sexual relations, and had been like that from birth. There were others who had been made incapable, quite deliberately. It was common, in some parts of the ancient world, for young slaves to be castrated, so that they could serve a royal or rich household without anyone worrying about them misbehaving with the womenfolk. And it was also recognized, though not without misgivings, that some people would choose not to marry so that they could devote themselves exclusively to God's work. **John the Baptist** was one such; Jesus himself, of course, was another.

These sayings may indeed have been cryptic because Jesus was aware that people might ask questions about his own marital status. The implication is that he has chosen to stay single because he is conscious of his extraordinary vocation and the demands it must make. When he says that some 'have made themselves eunuchs' in this sense, it's like the sayings in 18.8–9 about cutting off or plucking out hands, feet and eyes: he doesn't mean it literally. Of course, for some, the decision to postpone or renounce marriage seems every bit as hard as physical mutilation. And Jesus knows that God will not ask the same kinds of renunciation of all his servants. People who hear the call and find that they are able to follow it should do so. That's as far as one can go.

The whole discussion in Matthew 19.3–15 is of great relevance today. We live at a time when what used to be thought of as 'Christian' behaviour in the area of marriage and family has been rejected by large swathes of Western society – though upheld in many traditional cultures, including several explicitly non-Christian ones. The rampant individualism of the last few hundred years in the West has left families, and children, in bad shape, as people act on the belief that they have, as individuals, a 'right to happiness' which overrides all considerations of loyalty, keeping vows, and the duty to bring up lovingly the children one has brought into the world.

Nobody – certainly not Jesus – ever said that following him and finding God's kingdom-way in these matters would be easy. But nobody should imagine that it's just an optional extra. As Jesus comes closer to Jerusalem, and to his own astonishing act of self-denial and self-sacrifice, we should take note that the call to follow him extends to the most personal and intimate details of our lives.

MATTHEW 19.16–22

The Rich Young Man

| [16]Suddenly a man came up to Jesus. 'Teacher,' he asked, 'what |

good thing must I do if I'm to possess the life of the age to come?'

¹⁷'Why come to me with questions about what's good?' retorted Jesus. 'There is one who is good! If you want to enter into life, keep the commandments.'

¹⁸'Which ones?' he asked.

'These ones,' Jesus answered: '"don't murder, don't commit adultery, don't steal, don't tell lies under oath, ¹⁹respect your father and mother", and "love your neighbour as yourself"'.

²⁰'I've kept the lot,' said the young man. 'What am I still short of?'

²¹'If you want to complete the set,' Jesus replied, 'go and sell everything you own and give it to the poor. That way you'll have treasure in heaven! Then come and follow me.'

²²When the young man heard him say that, he went away very sad. He had many possessions.

I have heard it said that if you want to catch a monkey, there is a particular method which works well. You need a jar which the monkey can just get his paw into when his fingers are open. Then you put something into the jar which the monkey wants – some fruit, say. Then you put the jar temptingly where the monkey is likely to find it.

The monkey will reach his hand into the jar to get the fruit. He will close his fist around it. But of course, when he closes his fist, especially if it's got something inside it, he can't get it out of the jar. He won't want to let the fruit go, but unless he does he won't be able to get his hand out.

The story has an obvious meaning when we put it alongside Jesus' meeting with this eager young man. He had great possessions. He was probably well known; there weren't very many rich people in Jesus' world, and such as there were would be local figures of note. Lots of less rich people would be doing their best to make friends with him, or work for him, hoping that some of his wealth might find its way towards them. (That, incidentally, is only one of the ways in which wealth corrupts human relationships.) But he was like the monkey with his hand in the jar. He had a tight grip on his possessions, and unless he was prepared to loosen his grip and leave them behind he couldn't become free. He wouldn't be free to join the kingdom-movement, the march into God's future, that Jesus was leading.

He wasn't simply asking about how to go to **heaven** after he died. As we've seen often enough, the phrase '**kingdom of heaven**' doesn't mean that. It means God's sovereign, saving rule coming to transform everything, coming to bring the whole creation into a new state of being, a new life, in which evil, decay and death itself will be done away. Many, perhaps most, Jews of Jesus' day believed that Israel's God would do this, and would do it very soon. The question they were asking, in several different ways, was: who would benefit from it when it happened? Who would 'inherit the **age to come**'? Who would gain 'the life of the new age', or, as in many translations, '**eternal life**'?

The standard Jewish answer to this question would be something to do with keeping the Jewish **laws** – the commandments that God gave to Moses. Most serious-minded Jews of Jesus' day had their own opinions about what these laws demanded. Everyone knew the basic list, the Ten Commandments; the point was then to find out what exactly they meant in practice. Different groups had their different agendas. The **Pharisees** had some very detailed regulations; the **Essenes** had a different set; and so on.

Jesus was not offering simply another set of legal interpretations of that sort. His challenge was at a different level. He was content, in terms of behaviour, simply to repeat the basic commandments (though it's interesting that he doesn't mention the first four, about putting God first, getting rid of idols, not taking God's name in vain, and keeping the **sabbath**). He knows that the young man knows these, and the young man knows that he knows; both of them understand that the conversation must move to different ground, to the point where the real questions begin.

This is where Jesus' approach is different in kind from those of other Jewish groups. Instead of more complex legal instructions, he has the simplest of commands: sell up, give it away and follow me. There is something ironic about the way he says it here: 'If you want to complete the set . . .'. In Matthew, being 'complete' – the same word can mean 'perfect', actually! – is the challenge of the Sermon on the Mount (5.48). It's a way of saying, 'God wants his people to be complete, totally dedicated to his service, not half-and-half people, with one foot in the kingdom and the other in the world.' The young man seems to want almost to *collect* commandments he's kept, like one might collect coins or butterflies or antique furniture. All right, says Jesus, this is the one that will complete your collection: give everything away! In order to be complete, you must be empty. In order to have everything, you must have nothing. In order to be fully signed up to God's service, you must be signed off from everything else.

As with the previous comments about celibacy, this commandment was not given to everybody. Jesus doesn't often seem to have told people to give away everything and follow him. When he did, it was either because, as in the case of the **Twelve**, he wanted them to be free so that they could be with him all the time and share his work; or because, as with this young man, he sensed that his possessions had become his idol, his alternative god, the **demon** that would eventually kill him unless he renounced it.

We all have something like that in our lives. It may well not be material possessions: in our world, as in that of Jesus, not many people are very rich (even if most of them are concentrated in certain places). It is up to each of us to examine our own hearts and lives to see what is holding us back from serving God with the 'completeness' which Jesus longs for.

MATTHEW 19.23–30

The First and the Last

²³Jesus said to his disciples, 'I'm telling you the truth: it's very hard for a rich person to get into the kingdom of heaven. ²⁴Let me say it again: it's easier for a camel to go through the eye of a needle than for a rich person to enter God's kingdom.'

²⁵The disciples were completely flabbergasted when they heard that. 'So who then can be saved?' they asked.

Jesus looked round at them. 'Humanly speaking,' he replied, 'it's impossible. But everything's possible with God.'

²⁷Then Peter spoke up. 'Look here,' he said, 'we've left everything behind and followed you. What can we expect?'

'I'm telling you the truth,' Jesus replied. 'In God's great new world, when the son of man sits on his glorious throne, all of you who have followed me will sit on twelve thrones – yes, you! – and rule over the twelve tribes of Israel. ²⁹And anyone who's left houses or brothers or sisters or father or mother or children or estates because of my name will get back a hundred times over, and will inherit the life of that new age. ³⁰But many at the front will find themselves at the back, and the back ones at the front.'

Once, as a boy, I watched a large party of hunters on horseback chasing a fox over open country. Even if you disapprove of foxhunting, as many do, it was a fine sight on a cold wintry day. Down the hillside they came: in the front were the leaders, in red hunting uniform, on splendid horses. They were blowing horns, close behind the hounds, looking like what they were – the local gentry, landowners, the rich and well known. Behind them were other fine riders on good-quality horses, wearing brown and black hunting clothes. Behind them again, less orderly, on various types and sizes of horse, and without any real uniform except their ordinary country clothes, came a raggle-taggle group of riders, enjoying themselves but not such a fine sight.

But then, with typical cunning, the fox they were all pursuing hid in a thicket, and doubled back up the next field so that it suddenly reappeared near the top of the hill it had come from in the first place. One of the riders near the back of the pack spotted it, and blew a horn. And the whole company of riders had to turn round and go back the way they'd come.

That was the sight I remember. Leading the way, this time, were the raggle-taggle group of riders on whichever old horses they had managed to find. In the middle were the riders in brown and black. And right at the back, having got to the bottom of the long hill only to find they must turn round and go back, were the red-coated brigade, looking decidedly out of sorts and embarrassed at bringing up the rear, something they weren't used to doing either in hunting or in society.

Those at the back, said Jesus, will find themselves at the front, and those at the front will find themselves at the back. There will be astonishment, embarrassment, delight and dismay. God is going to stand everything on its head. In the long human hunt for truth, wisdom, justice and salvation, the divine fox has doubled back, and is reappearing where we least expected him. This time, the nobodies are in the lead, and the great and good are in the rear.

That is Jesus' verdict on the sorry episode of the rich young man, which the **disciples** then discuss with him. We should notice how amazed they were to be told that rich people would have difficulty getting into God's **kingdom**. They had taken it for granted that, if God had made his kingdom so that Israel, in particular, could inherit it, those who were rich and famous in Israel would certainly be guaranteed a place.

In our world, television and magazines can make people 'celebrities' on very slender grounds. People often regard rock stars, fashion icons, movie actors and sports heroes with an awe they used to reserve for royalty, or even for God. The results are plain to see, when such people turn out to have very ordinary human lives and emotions which can't take the strain that fame produces. In Jesus' world, many regarded God's promises of blessing in the Old Testament as meaning that those who seemed to have the greatest blessings in the present – in other words, the rich, titled and landed – must be God's favourites. It came as a great shock to be told otherwise. They were among the people 'at the front', who would probably end up 'at the back'.

Some people have suggested that the saying about the camel going through the eye of a needle is actually a reference to a gate in Jerusalem that was called 'the needle's eye'. A camel would need to unload all it was carrying on its back to get through it. Other people have pointed out that a word very similar to 'camel' meant a sort of rope; maybe he was talking of threading a sailor's rope through a seamstress's needle. But both of these suggestions miss the point. As we have seen in this chapter and the previous ones, Jesus often exaggerates hugely to make his point. It's like saying, 'You couldn't get a Rolls-Royce into a matchbox.' The point is not that you might achieve it if you tried very hard, or that there was a particular type of small garage called a 'matchbox'; the point is precisely that it's unthinkable. That's the moment when all human calculations and possibilities stop, and God's new possibilities start. What is impossible in human terms, Jesus' followers are to discover to their amazement, is possible to God (verse 26).

Jesus is then offering a vision of God's whole new world in which everything will be upside down and inside out. He uses pictures we have become accustomed to in the **gospel** story. The **son of man** sitting on his glorious throne takes us to chapter 7 of the prophetic book of Daniel, where God's kingdom will be established at last with the overthrow of evil and the vindication of God's people. Then those who have given up everything to follow Jesus will find themselves not only rescued from eternal death, but actually ruling with Jesus himself in the new world.

He speaks of the **Twelve**, and of their twelve thrones. It is probable that the Twelve themselves thought he meant this literally. They were soon to find that one of their number would turn traitor, and that the central throne in the whole picture was not the normal kind, but consisted of two planks of wood and four nails. The fate that was waiting for Jesus in Jerusalem would underline, in the starkest way possible, that God's new world comes through the complete reversal of all normal ideas of kingship and earthly greatness.

MATTHEW 20.1–16

The Workers in the Vineyard

[1]'So you see,' Jesus continued, 'the kingdom of heaven is like a landowner who went out early in the morning to hire workers for his vineyard. [2]He agreed with the workers to give them a pound a day, and sent them off to his vineyard.

[3]'He went out again in the middle of the morning, and saw some others standing in the marketplace with nothing to do.

[4]"You too can go to the vineyard," he said, "and I'll give you what's right." [5]So off they went.

'He went out again about midday, and then in the middle of the afternoon, and did the same. [6]Then, with only an hour of the day left, he went out and found other people standing there.

'"Why are you standing here all day with nothing to do?" he asked them.

[7]"Because no one has hired us," they replied.

'"Well," he said, "you too can go into the vineyard."

⁸'When evening came, the vineyard-owner said to his servant, "Call the workers and give them their pay. Start with the last, and go on to the first."

⁹'So the ones who had worked for one hour came, and each of them received a pound. ¹⁰When the first ones came, they thought they would get something more; but they, too, each received a pound.

¹¹'When they had been given it, they grumbled against the landowner. ¹²"This lot who came in last", they said, "have only worked for one hour – and they've been put on a level with us! And we did all the hard work, all day, and in the heat as well!"

¹³'"My friend," he said to one of them, "I'm not doing you any wrong. You agreed with me on one pound, didn't you? ¹⁴Take it! It's yours! And be on your way. I want to give this fellow who came at the end the same as you. ¹⁵Or are you suggesting that I'm not allowed to do what I like with my own money? Or are you giving me the evil eye because I'm good?"

¹⁶'So those at the back will be at the front, and the front ones at the back.'

One of the great inventions of modern Western society is the trade union. For far too long those with money, land and privilege shamelessly exploited those who had none. When, after a long struggle, workers with no power except their own labour managed to stand together and force the issue with the rich and strong, it was a great day for freedom and justice.

But over the course of the twentieth century things changed. Exploitation and injustice often continued, and the unions often did a fine job in checking or reversing it. But other issues came into the picture, and made life more complicated, more morally ambiguous. In many Western countries now, the role of the unions has become quite different from what their founders envisaged. In some cases this has been for the better; in others, in my judgment, for the worse.

One of the ways in which some unions have changed from

their original purpose is that they have often set workers against one another. They have insisted on different pay for different jobs, even if the employers had other ideas. Such unions would have been horrified at the story Jesus told about this employer and the workers who laboured, some for the whole day, others for part, and others again for only the last hour. Indeed, we are not surprised when, in the story, the workers themselves grumbled. Where is the sense of fairness, of justice, in paying the last workers the same as the first?

It's important to realize that Jesus doesn't intend the story to serve as a comment on the social justice of his day. How likely such an incident is to have happened we can only guess, but most people who have studied that world think it is very *un*likely. Jesus is accepting, for the purpose of the story, the social and economic power of the landowner, in order to say something about God; what he would say to rich landowners themselves, then and now, may be guessed from chapter 19.

But what is he saying about God, and why is he saying it here? To answer this we need to look a bit more closely at the last group of workers, the ones who were hired when only one hour of the day was left. It is curious, we may suppose, that they hadn't been spotted before. Had they not been in the marketplace earlier? The vineyard-owner questions them: why haven't you been working? Their answer is revealing: nobody has hired us, nobody has given us a job. Nobody, in other words, wanted them. They were, perhaps, the sort of people everybody tried not to hire.

But the landowner hired them, and paid them the same as the people who had been slaving away all day in the heat of the sun. As in so many of Jesus' stories, the landowner is obviously standing for God, and the workers for Israel. Who are the different categories of workers meant to represent?

Jesus probably intends the **parable** as a warning to the **disciples** themselves about their own attitudes. When he said, at the end of the previous chapter, that those at the front would end up at the back, and vice versa, it may have seemed that 'those at the front' was referring to the rich and powerful, and that 'those at the back' meant the disciples themselves. However, that saying was part of the answer to Peter, after his somewhat self-centred question in 19.27 ('We've left everything and followed you; so what is our reward?'). It's possible that, already in chapter 19, Jesus is intending the riddling saying about first and last, the front and the back, to be a warning to the disciples themselves: don't think that, because you've been close to me so far, you are now the favoured few for all time.

That, I believe, is the main thrust of this story in chapter 20. It goes only too well, when we read it like this, with the rest of the chapter, which is a warning to the disciples about the danger they are in, supposing that, because Jesus is bringing in the **kingdom of heaven**, they are going to become rich and famous in their turn. That's not the sort of thing, Jesus warns them, that God's kingdom is about. They may have set out with Jesus from the very beginning; but others may well come in much later and end up getting paid just the same, the regular daily wage (I have used 'pound' here to translate *denarius*, which was the regular daily wage for a manual labourer).

God's grace, in short, is not the sort of thing you can bargain with or try to store up. It isn't the sort of thing that one person can have a lot of and someone else only a little. The point of the story is that what people get from having served God and his kingdom is not, actually, a 'wage' at all. It's not, strictly, a reward for work done. God doesn't make contracts with us, as if we could bargain or negotiate for a better deal. He makes **covenants**, in which he promises us everything and asks of us everything in return. When he keeps his promises, he is not rewarding us for effort, but doing what comes naturally to his overflowingly generous nature.

There is always a danger that we get cross with God over

this. People who work in church circles can easily assume that they are the special ones, God's inner circle. In reality, God is out in the marketplace, looking for the people everybody else tried to ignore, welcoming them on the same terms, surprising them (and everybody else) with his generous grace. The earliest church clearly needed to learn that lesson. Is there anywhere in today's church that doesn't need to be reminded of it as well?

MATTHEW 20.17–28

The Cup He Had to Drink

[17]Jesus was on his way up to Jerusalem. He took the twelve disciples aside in private, while they were on the road, and said to them,

[18]'Look here. We're going up to Jerusalem. The son of man will be handed over to the chief priests and the scribes, and they're going to condemn him to death. [19]They will hand him over to the pagans, and they're going to make fun of him, and torture him, and crucify him. And on the third day he will be raised.'

[20]Then the mother of Zebedee's sons came up, with her sons, to Jesus. She bowed low in front of him and indicated that she had a special request to make.

[21]'What d'you want?' he asked her.

'It's about these two sons of mine,' she said to him. 'Please say that, when you're king, they may sit, one at your right hand and one at your left.'

[22]'You don't know what you're asking for,' said Jesus. 'Can you two drink the cup I'm going to drink?'

'Yes, we can,' they replied.

[23]'Well,' said Jesus, 'so you will drink my cup, then! But sitting at my right and left is not something I can grant. That's up to my father to give to whoever he has in mind.'

[24]When the other ten heard this they were annoyed with the two brothers. [25]But Jesus called them together.

'You know how it is with pagan rulers,' he said. 'They lord

it over their subjects. They get all high and mighty and let everybody know it. [26]But that's not how it's to be with you. If any of you wants to be great, he must be your servant. [27]If any of you wants to be first, he must be the slave of all. [28]That's how it is with the son of man: he didn't come to have servants obey him, but to *be* a servant – and to give his life as "a ransom for many".

When I was a boy we used to read eagerly about the heroes of old. One of the most famous was King Arthur, a British king from the early sixth century. We had plenty of books that told stories about him, and you can go and see his various castles, like the spectacular one at Tintagel in Cornwall. But there isn't actually much known about him that will pass as serious history. Most of it comes to us through legend, poetry, song and (frankly) romantic wishful thinking.

However, one of the most important stories about Arthur, and about the knights that sat at his famous Round Table, still carries power today. It's about their quest for the Holy Grail – the cup that Jesus supposedly used at the Last Supper. In this cup, according to legend, Joseph of Arimathea (whom we shall meet in Matthew 27.57) had then caught Jesus' blood as it drained from his body on the cross. Another legend suggested that Joseph had brought the cup to Britain. Somehow it had become lost; but the knights were determined to find it, and their quest then became a great act of devotion, loyalty and courage.

The idea of a quest to find Jesus' cup goes all the way back to passages like this one in the New Testament – where we find that Jesus stands on their heads all the usual ideas about royalty, nobility and the like. This isn't the last time we shall meet the idea of a 'cup' from which Jesus must drink, and it's important that we get clear at this stage what it's all about.

At the heart of the story (throughout these chapters, but

here in particular) is the head-on clash between what Jesus is trying to explain to the **disciples** and what they assume their journey to Jerusalem is all about. They are so convinced that he must really be following the sort of plan they have in mind that they simply can't register his repeated warnings that it's all going to be very different. He is talking about dying a horrible death, and they seem to think it's just picture-language for the great victory he's going to win. (So, in a sense, it is; but not at all in the way they think.)

James and John come with their mother to Jesus. She's had a bright idea (or perhaps it was theirs all along): when Jesus sits on his throne, as they all know he's going to do, why not have her two sons on either side of him?

This request opens a window for us on the whole sordid business of power. Young politicians try to guess who's going to be powerful. They attach themselves to him or her, so that if they've guessed right they will be rewarded handsomely for their early allegiance. People play games like that all the time. It produces cheap 'loyalty' that's not worth a thing, hollow 'friendships' that don't go deeper than the outward smile, and easy betrayals when things go wrong. That's the level the two brothers were working at. When the other disciples are cross with them, it's probably not because they were all too pure-minded to have similar thoughts, but simply because James and John got in first.

Jesus' curious answer to them opens a very different window: on the biblical roots of the calling which he was following. The Old Testament prophets speak darkly about the 'cup of **YHWH**'s wrath' (Isaiah 51.17, 22; Jeremiah 25.15–29; and several other passages). These passages talk of what happens when the one God, grieving over the awful wickedness of the world, steps in at last to give the violent and bloodthirsty, the arrogant and oppressors, the reward for their ways and deeds. It's as though God's holy anger against such people is turned into wine: dark, sour wine which will make them drunk and helpless. They will be forced to 'drink the cup', to drain to the dregs the wrath of the God who loves and vindicates the weak and helpless.

The shock of this passage – and it becomes more shocking as we go forward from here – is that Jesus speaks of drinking this cup himself. No wonder the disciples couldn't grasp the idea! They were eager to become rich and famous themselves. They were bent on power, position and prestige. They were becoming . . . yes, just a little bit like the arrogant, the rulers of the world, the people the **gospel** was meant to overthrow. Had they, so soon, forgotten the Sermon on the Mount?

Jesus rams the lesson home with another biblical allusion, from two chapters further on in Isaiah (53.10–12). There is a biblical model for the kind of kingship he has in mind, and it's the one which sees the king as the servant, giving his life as a 'ransom for many'.

A 'ransom', in that world, is what someone might pay to give freedom to a slave. Jesus saw his approaching fate as the payment that would set free those who were enslaved in sin and wickedness, not least those who were in the grips of the lust for power and position – yes, people like James and John.

The original Quest for the Holy Grail, then, was Jesus' own calling: to follow God's leading, as indicated in scripture, to the point of death. James and John might indeed suffer the same fate in their turn (James was killed quite early in the Christian movement, according to Acts 12.2). When Jesus was enthroned as King of Israel there would indeed be one at his right and one at his left (27.38). But what they would be sharing was not glory and power but shame and death.

MATTHEW 20.29–34

The Healing of Two Blind Men

| ²⁹As they were going out of Jericho, a large crowd was following |

61

Jesus. [30]Just then two blind men were sitting by the wayside, and heard that Jesus was going by. 'Have pity on us, master, son of David!' they shouted.

[31]The crowd scolded them and told them to be silent. But they shouted out all the more, 'Have pity on us, master, son of David!'

[32]Jesus came to a stop. He called them.

'What d'you want me to do for you?' he asked.

[33]'Master,' they replied, 'we want you to open our eyes.'

[34]Jesus was very moved. He touched their eyes. At once they could see again, and they followed him.

He came to see me early in the morning. He was a bit nervous at telling a clergyman how he was feeling, but he was determined to do it anyway.

He told me he hadn't been able to sleep too well the last few nights. He had a sense that his work wasn't going too well; his heart didn't seem to be in it. He was restless and couldn't figure out why. For the last few years he'd devoted himself single-mindedly to the grand scheme he'd worked out. He would get a degree, study for an MBA, find the right company, start off up the business ladder. Now here he was, halfway through, on the road to success. And yet something wasn't right.

'Richard,' I said, feeling it was a rather silly question, 'what do you *really* want to do?'

He stared at me for a moment with a mixture of horror and amazement. It was like watching a dam burst. The emotion and energy that had built up inside him came flooding through in a rush. 'What I *really* want to do', he said, 'is to get ordained and tell people about Jesus!' He blushed to the roots of his hair as though this was the most stupid thing an MBA student could possibly say. He had the world at his feet. Why change course and go off into the unknown? Surely he wasn't going to become one of those professional religious types? Surely God could use him as a businessman, without him giving it all up?

But he had spoken the truth, and we both knew it. This was what he really wanted. It was a huge thing, but the way was now clear.

Jesus asked the same question to the two blind men outside Jericho. It may sound an obvious question and answer to us, but it was by no means obvious to them, or to the crowds.

Think about it. In many cities around today's world, you will see people sitting by the roadside saying the same words to everyone who passes by: 'Spare a thought for an old woman!' 'Got a few coins, sir?' 'Take pity on an old soldier!' 'Can you spare some change, mister?' On and on, day after day.

Try to see the world through their eyes . . . You get used to people ignoring you, or smiling patronizingly. You get used to some people stopping to talk, then moving on with a mixture of embarrassment and pity. You get used to sitting there, in cold and heat, hoping for just enough coins to get through the next day, and the next, and the next. Maybe you have a few friends, relatives even, in the same plight, and from time to time you get together with what little you've made from a day or two on the street. It's not much of a life, but it's the one you know.

It's the one these two blind men knew. They had each other for company, and no doubt all the travellers through Jericho had seen them dozens of times. They probably had family in the town, eking out a bare existence. This was where they belonged.

So when they heard that Jesus was coming through they pricked up their ears. For James and John, in the previous passage, the thought that Jesus was going to be king meant that perhaps they would get to sit on either side of him. For two blind beggars outside Jericho, the thought that Jesus, the **son of David**, was coming through town meant . . . money. Where there's royalty, there's riches. If anyone can give us enough to live on for a while, surely he can. Then we won't have to go on with this begging day after day.

So they redouble their efforts, despite the crowd's attempts to shut them up. 'Have pity on us, son of David, have pity!' 'Mercy for a blind man!' 'Son of David, be kind to us!' Call him a king, that'll make him feel good, make him want to show how generous he is – the rich like to give money when lots of people are watching . . .

Perhaps the most they hoped for was that Jesus would send one of his minions across to them with some coins. They certainly didn't expect him to call them. They had to get up from their regular seats and come over to him. They heard the noisy crowd go suddenly quiet. They were on the spot. Everyone must be watching them. And the voice that had called them, the voice they guessed must be Jesus, was asking them a question nobody had asked them for years and years . . .

'What do you want me to do for you?'

Well . . . what d'you think? What does a beggar always want? But . . . why was he asking? What did he mean? Was he hinting . . . ? But they'd look very stupid if they asked and he couldn't, or wouldn't – and then they wouldn't get the money either . . . perhaps it would be better to play safe, stick with the trade they knew?

We watch them there in the hot Jericho sun. The few seconds must have seemed like hours. Then the dam burst.

'Master – open our eyes! That's what we want! Open our eyes!'

Jesus, says Matthew, was deeply moved. He had watched the human drama that had taken place in those few moments. He knew what it had cost them, and would cost them, to dig down beneath the hard crust of a lifetime of begging for money and to ask instead for the one thing that really mattered. He touched them, and they saw.

And, says Matthew, they followed him. Well, they would,

wouldn't they? But we know, as they do not yet, what that means. They have left one life behind, and have begun a new one. It can happen to anyone who asks Jesus for something and finds Jesus' searching question coming straight back at them, piercing through the outer crust and finding the real request bubbling up underneath.

And when that real request is really met, the only possible result is real discipleship. Following Jesus will be costly. But if he's already given you everything you really wanted, what else is there to do?

MATTHEW 21.1–11

Jesus Rides into Jerusalem

¹When they came near to Jerusalem, and arrived at Bethphage on the Mount of Olives, Jesus sent two of the disciples on ahead.

²'Go into the village over there,' he said, 'and at once you'll find a donkey tied up, and a foal beside it. Untie them and bring them to me. ³And if anyone says anything to you, say, "The Master needs them."'

He sent them off at once.

⁴This happened so that the prophet's words might be fulfilled:

⁵Tell this to Zion's daughter:
Look now! Here comes your king;
He's humble, mounted on an ass,
Yes, on a foal, its young.

⁶So the disciples went off and did as Jesus had told them. ⁷They brought the donkey and its foal, and put their cloaks on them, and Jesus sat on them.

⁸The huge crowd spread their cloaks on the road. Others cut branches from the trees and scattered them on the road. ⁹The

crowds who went on ahead of him, and those who were following behind, shouted out,

> Hosanna now to David's Son!
> God's blessing on the coming one!
> Hosanna in the highest!

[10]When they came into Jerusalem, the whole city was gripped with excitement.

'Who is this?' they were saying.

[11]'This is the prophet, Jesus,' replied the crowds, 'from Nazareth in Galilee!'

There is a famous story of Sir Walter Raleigh, one of the great explorers and travellers during the reigns of Queen Elizabeth I and King James I of England. On one occasion he was with the queen when she was walking through London, and came to a place where rainwater had made the ground muddy and dirty. He quickly took off his cloak and placed it on the ground so the queen could walk over without getting mud on her feet.

The tale may or may not be true – though for some years Raleigh certainly was Elizabeth's great favourite – but it illustrates the point of this incident. The story of Raleigh taking off his cloak has become famous, partly because it's not the sort of thing that happens every day. If it has occurred in my lifetime, for princes, presidents, or Prime Ministers, I've never heard of it. It's a very special gesture, especially if (as was probably not the case for Raleigh) the cloak is the only one you've got. It says, quite clearly, that you are celebrating and valuing this person about as highly as you can. It implies that, if need arose, you would give them anything else you had as well.

Most of the crowd around Jesus probably didn't have a second cloak, but they spread theirs on the road anyway. Those who knew their Bibles might have remembered that when one of Israel's famous kings of old was proclaimed king in defiance of the existing one, his followers spread their cloaks under his feet as a sign of loyalty (2 Kings 9.13). They were determined to make a statement about what they thought was going on.

They also waved the branches they'd cut from the trees to make a celebratory procession for him. This too carried 'royal' implications. In the long folk-memory of Jerusalem and its surrounding villages, stories were still told, and some of them by this stage were written down, about the famous Judas Maccabaeus who, 200 years before, had arrived in Jerusalem after conquering the pagan armies that had oppressed Israel. He, too, was welcomed into the city by a crowd waving palm branches (2 Maccabees 10.7). And he was the start of a royal dynasty that lasted for over a hundred years. Indeed, the Herod family had intermarried with the Maccabaean family, and the chief **priests** claimed a similar status.

To add to the effect, they sang 'royal' hymns or chants. Welcoming Jesus as '**son of David**' was about as explicit as you could get; this was, after all, the city which King David had made his capital a thousand years before, and for nearly half that time the Jews had been waiting and praying for a king like David to arrive and save them from oppression. Surely, they thought, this was the moment! The whole procession was saying, in its way, what James and John and their mother had been saying in their way in the previous chapter. Jesus is going to be the sort of king we want! Let's make that quite clear!

But Jesus knows, and Matthew has told us, that nothing is that simple. We know that he has come to Jerusalem, not to be enthroned like David, or like Judas Maccabaeus, or like Herod, but to be killed. The meaning Jesus attaches to this so-called 'triumphal entry' is quite different from the meaning they are wanting to see in it. That, perhaps, is where we can learn most from this story today.

People turn to God, notoriously, when there is something they want very badly. Of course, that's like finally deciding to learn to use a telephone only when you urgently need to call an ambulance; it would have been sensible to find out how to do it earlier, when it wasn't so important. But that's how people are. Church attendance goes up in leaps and bounds when a major crisis strikes – a war, say, or an earthquake. Suddenly everyone wants to ask the big, hard questions. Suddenly everyone wants Jesus, in terms of this story, to ride into the city and become the sort of king they want him to be. Give us peace, now! Pay my bills, and hurry! Save the life of my sick child, and do it right away! Give me a job by this time tomorrow! And – perhaps the most common prayer of all – Help!

Jesus intends to answer these and all other prayers. He doesn't wait for our motives to be pure, or for us to have sorted out our lives to the point where we can look him in the face, eye to eye as it were, and do business with him. Of course he doesn't. He has come to seek and rescue the lost. It isn't the healthy who need the doctor, but the sick.

However, at the same time he must answer in his own way. The people wanted a prophet, but this prophet would tell them that their city was under God's imminent judgment (chapter 24). They wanted a **Messiah**, but this one was going to be enthroned on a pagan cross. They wanted to be rescued from evil and oppression, but Jesus was going to rescue them from evil in its full depths, not just the surface evil of Roman occupation and the exploitation by the rich. Precisely because Jesus says 'yes' to their desires at the deepest level, he will have to say 'no' or 'wait' to the desires they are conscious of, and expressed.

That's the funny thing with prayer. Once you invite Jesus to help, he will do so more thoroughly than you imagined, more deeply than perhaps you wanted. If you invite an accountant to help you with your income tax return, you mustn't be surprised if she goes through all your other financial affairs as well, to make sure she's got everything right.

The story of Jesus' grand, though surprising, entry into Jerusalem, then, is an object lesson in the mismatch between our expectations and God's answer (compare 16.23, where Jesus says something like this to Peter). The bad news is that the crowds are going to be disappointed. But the good news is that their disappointment, though cruel, is at the surface level. Deep down, Jesus' arrival at the great city is indeed the moment when salvation is dawning. The 'Hosannas' were justified, though not for the reasons they had supposed. To learn this lesson is to take a large step towards wisdom and humility, and towards genuine Christian **faith**.

MATTHEW 21.12–22

The Temple and the Fig-Tree

¹²Jesus went into the Temple and threw out all the people who were buying and selling in the Temple. He upturned the tables of the money-changers and the seats of the dove-sellers.

¹³'This is what the Bible says,' he said to them,

My house will be called a house of prayer –
But you have made it a brigands' lair!'

¹⁴The blind and the lame came to him in the Temple, and he healed them. ¹⁵But when the chief priests and the scribes saw the remarkable things he was doing, and the children shouting out 'Hosanna to David's son!' in the Temple, they were very cross.

¹⁶'Do you hear what they're saying?' they asked Jesus.

'Yes,' said Jesus. 'Did you never read what it says,

You called forth praise to rise to you
From newborn babes and infants too!

[17]Then he left them, and went out of the city to Bethany, where he stayed the night.

[18]Early the next morning Jesus went back to the city. He was hungry. [19]He saw a single fig-tree beside the road, but when he came up to it he found nothing on it except leaves.

'May nobody eat your fruit ever again!' he said to it. Instantly the fig-tree withered up.

[20]The disciples saw it, and were astonished.

'Look how quickly the fig-tree has withered up!' they said.

[21]'I'm telling you the truth,' replied Jesus. 'If you have faith, and don't doubt, you will not only be able to do this to a fig-tree, but if you say to this mountain, "Be lifted up and thrown into the sea", it will happen. [22]Whatever you ask in prayer, you'll get it, if you believe.'

Once upon a time there was a king who wanted to give his country a new lease of life. He decided to capture a city that none of his people had lived in before, and make it his capital, so that no one would feel either proud that their city had been chosen, or excluded because it was someone else's.

The problem was that the city was perched high on a rocky crag, and was very easy to defend against attack. (That, of course, was another reason for wanting it.) The inhabitants saw this upstart king coming with his army, and knew they'd have no trouble warding him off. So sure were they that they sent him a message: 'All the regular guards have gone off duty. We've put the blind ones on watch and told the lame ones to take the messages – they'll do the job all right!'

But the king knew a better trick than that. He knew that however strongly a city was built on a hill, it needed one thing: water. And he'd discovered where the spring of water rose. That was the way in! So he set his men a challenge: get up the water shaft and fight your way in. First one up will be my new general! So up they went and took the city. And it did indeed become his capital.

But he didn't forget the scorn of the local people, and what they'd said about the blind and the lame keeping him out. So he made it a rule: no blind and lame welcome here. No reminders, please, of the mocking of the enemy.

The king was, of course, King David; the city was, of course, Jerusalem; and the house where the blind and the lame were not welcome was, of course, the **Temple**. The story is told in 2 Samuel 5.6–10 and 1 Chronicles 11.4–6. And now we are ready to see what Matthew is doing in telling the story of how King Jesus came to Jerusalem, and to the Temple, a thousand years later.

Jesus did with the Temple's traditions what he did with the money-changers' tables: he turned them upside down. Matthew is the only **gospel** to mention this, but with the story of David in our heads we can't miss the point in verse 14: the blind and the lame came to Jesus in the Temple, *and he healed them*. The people who had been kept out were now welcomed in. The people who had been scorned were now healed. It was an action full of significance. It summed up everything Jesus had been doing throughout his ministry.

It was flanked, of course, by two other actions, both of them equally powerful. But what did they mean?

Jesus wasn't trying to take over the Temple by force, as some people have thought. Nor was he making a protest about exploitation by the money-changers and the dove-sellers. They may well have been making a profit; they, after all, had to make a living as well as everybody else. People needed to be able to buy pure animals for **sacrifice**; if you tried to bring a dove or a sheep from Galilee all the way to Jerusalem, it might well be killed or maimed on the way. To buy animals you needed the right money, and the Temple insisted on its own special coins. The sacrificial system had been ordained by God; that's what the Temple was there for, to link Israel to God day by day and hour by hour in the ceaseless round of worship. And Jesus is implying that something has gone badly wrong with it.

It isn't the buying, selling and money-changing he's objecting to in itself. When he says, 'You've made it a brigands' lair', the word *brigand* doesn't mean a thief. 'Brigands' were revolutionaries, people who believed so strongly in God's coming **kingdom** of justice and triumph for Israel they were prepared to take the law into their own hands. They were the violent ones Jesus had commented on earlier in the gospel (11.12). The Temple itself, instead of being regarded as the place where Israel could come to God in prayer, had come to stand for the violent longings of the 'brigands' for a great revolution in which the kingdom of God would come by force. It was everything Jesus had opposed throughout his lifetime, not least in the Sermon on the Mount. Now his warnings against 'the house' were to come true.

How might he best demonstrate that, in a powerful symbolic protest? By stopping the sacrificial system. If people couldn't change money or buy doves, even for a short while, they couldn't offer sacrifice. The Temple's reason for existence was called into question. The healing of the blind and the lame said the same, in a softer mode. The ideology that had sustained Jerusalem, that of military might and conquest, would suffice no longer.

This, too, is the reason for Jesus' otherwise apparently petulant action with the fig-tree. He came looking for fruit, but when he found none he solemnly declared that the tree would be barren for ever. That's exactly what he was doing with the Temple. And the promise to the **disciples**, which follows from it, is not a general comment about the power of prayer to do extraordinary things (though of course it is true that all sorts of things can be accomplished through prayer). The promise is far more focused than that. Saying to 'this mountain' that it should be 'lifted up and thrown into the sea', when you are standing right beside the Temple mountain, was bound to be taken as another coded warning about what would happen to the Temple as God's judgment fell upon his rebellious people.

Suddenly, therefore, the lines of Jesus' work all through the earlier days in Galilee come together with a new force. All along he'd been acting as if you could get, by coming to him, the blessings you'd normally get by going to the Temple. Now he is declaring, in powerful actions, that the Temple itself is under God's judgment. We shall see in the following chapters what this will mean. The warnings become clearer still. The head-on conflict between Jesus and the Temple reaches its climax in the confrontation between the prophet from Galilee and the Temple's own ruler, the **high priest.**

But for the moment we should ponder not only Jesus' extraordinary and unique action, but the ways in which a similar revolution may sometimes be necessary in today's world. Which institutions in your country have become corrupt, so that they now serve the opposite purpose from that for which they were set up? Where do you see systems which were supposed to enable people to worship and pray, but which have now turned themselves in the opposite direction to the **message** of Jesus? What can you do about it?

MATTHEW 21.23–32

The Question about John

²³Jesus went into the Temple. As he was teaching, the chief priests and the elders of the people came up to him.

'By what right are you doing these things?' they asked him. 'Who gave you this right?'

²⁴'I'm going to ask you one question, too,' replied Jesus, 'and if you tell me the answer then I'll tell you by what right I'm doing these things. ²⁵Where did John's baptism come from? Was it from heaven, or from this world?'

They debated this among themselves. 'If we say "from heaven", they said, 'he's going to say to us, "So why didn't you believe him?" [26]But if we say "from this world", we'll have to watch out for the crowd, because they all reckon that John was a prophet.'

[27]So they answered Jesus, 'We don't know.'

'Well, then,' said Jesus, 'nor will I tell you by what right I'm doing these things.'

[28]'What d'you think?' he went on. 'Once upon a time there was a man who had two sons.

'He went to the first one and said, "Now then, my boy, off you go and do a day's work in the vineyard."

[29]"'Don't want to," replied the son; but afterwards he thought better of it and went.

[30]'He went to the other son and said the same thing.

"'Certainly, Master," he said; but he didn't go.

[31]'So which of the two did what his father wanted?'

'The first,' they answered.

'I'm telling you the truth,' Jesus said to them. 'The tax-collectors and prostitutes are going into God's kingdom ahead of you! [32]Yes: John came to you, in accordance with God's covenant plan, and you didn't believe him – but the tax-collectors and prostitutes believed him. But when you saw it, you didn't think better of it afterwards and believe him.'

When the police finally caught up with the man, they took him off to a police station and sat him down. They let him get his breath back, and then the questions began. 'What were you doing in that street at that time of night? What right did you have to be in that house? Where had you come from? Who did you see? Why were you so worried when we came to find you?'

But of course the question they really wanted to ask was: '*Did you commit the murder?*'

They couldn't ask it yet, because they didn't want to say the words too soon. If the suspect wasn't the murderer, but knew something about it, this might give the game away. If he was the murderer, a direct question would certainly make him say 'No', and then everything else would be useless. They needed to come with a barrage of other questions to get him talking, to get him either telling the truth or twisting around in so many lies that they'd catch him out sooner or later. Then the truth would come out.

The question the chief **priests** and the elders of the people really wanted to ask Jesus was: '*So do you think you're the Messiah?*' All the other questions they ask him, in this chapter and the next one, and all Jesus' answers, are whirling around this central issue. Why?

The answer is this: it was the Messiah who would have authority over the **Temple**. Jesus, let's face it, had walked in and had behaved as though he owned the place. Here he was, a country boy from Galilee, coming to the big, smart capital city. He walked into its holiest shrine, which had been ruled for centuries by the chief priests. And, for a moment, he took it over. Who did he think he was?

The only person who might conceivably have greater authority in the Temple than the high priest was God's anointed king, the Messiah – if and when he showed up. Nobody knew when that would be. Other would-be messiahs had come and gone. Now here was Jesus behaving as though he had the right to do what only the Messiah could do. So, naturally, they ask him: by what right are you doing all this? And who gave you this right?

Jesus' reply is a master-stroke. It both is and isn't a straight answer. It certainly isn't just a trick, designed to get them muddled or embarrassed, though it succeeded in doing that as well. Imagine the crowd all around, watching what could turn into a police investigation or arrest turning instead into a high-pressure and high-profile public debate, with the upstart from the country leaving the sophisticated city folk mumbling that they don't know the answer to his question.

Jesus' question about **John the Baptist** puts them on the spot, so that whichever answer they give they will be in trouble. But that's not all. The question about John is the clue to the answer Jesus could make, but doesn't yet, to their question. Matthew's reader knows that Jesus had already been anointed (in Hebrew, 'messiahed') by God, with the **holy spirit**, through John's **baptism** (3.16–17). That is where he was first declared to be God's beloved **son**, in other words, the Messiah. If the Jewish leaders truly understood what John had been doing, they would know where Jesus got the right to behave as Messiah in the Temple courts.

But Jesus isn't finished. He presses home his advantage. They may not believe that John was a prophet; but, supposing he was, what follows? Some people did what John said, even though they looked like rebels against God; other people refused to do what John said, even though they looked like God's chosen ones. Yes: just like two sons, one of whom said 'No' to his father but then did what had been asked, the other of whom said 'Yes' but then didn't do it.

Just in case they don't get the point, Jesus rubs it in. The first son, who rudely tells his father he doesn't feel like working today, but then does after all, stands for the tax-collectors and prostitutes. Their daily life seemed to be saying 'No' to God; but when they heard John they changed their mind and their lifestyle (in other words, they 'repented'). The second son, who politely tells his father he will indeed go to work, but then doesn't, stands for the Temple hierarchy and other leaders. They look as though they're doing God's will, worshipping in the Temple and keeping up appearances; but they refused to believe in John's message, not only about **repentance** but also about the Messiah who was standing unknown in their midst. Now the Messiah himself is here to call them to account. Not surprisingly, they don't like it.

The challenge of this passage for us today is partly this: to make sure we are responding to Jesus, allowing him to confront us at any point where we have been like the second son and said 'Yes' to God while in fact going off in the other direction. That's important, but it's not the only important thing. What we should also be asking is this. What should Jesus' followers be doing today that would challenge the powers of the present world with the news that he is indeed its rightful Lord? What should we be doing that would make people ask, 'By what right are you doing that?', to which the proper answer would be to tell, not now riddles about John the Baptist, but stories about Jesus himself?

MATTHEW 21.33–46

The Parable of the Tenants

[33]'Listen to another parable,' Jesus went on. 'Once upon a time there was a householder who planted a vineyard, built a wall for it, dug out a wine-press in it, and built a tower. Then he let it out to tenant farmers and went away on a journey.

[34]'When harvest time arrived, he sent his slaves to the farmers to collect his produce. [35]The farmers seized his slaves; they beat one, killed another, and stoned another. [36]Again he sent other slaves, more than before, and they treated them in the same way. [37]Finally he sent his son to them.

'"They'll respect my son," he said.

[38]'But the farmers saw the son.

'"This fellow's the heir!" they said to themselves. "Come on, let's kill him, and then we can take over the property!"

[39]'So they seized him, threw him out of the vineyard, and killed him.

[40]'Now then: when the vineyard-owner returns, what will he do to those farmers?'

[41]'He'll kill them brutally, the wretches!' they said. 'And he'll lease the vineyard to other farmers who'll give him the produce at the right time.'

[42]'Did you never read what the Bible says?' said Jesus to them:

The stone the builders threw away
Is now atop the corner;
It's from the Lord, all this, they say
And we looked on in wonder.

[43]'So let me tell you this: God's kingdom is going to be taken away from you and given to a nation that will produce the goods. [44]Anyone who falls on this stone will be smashed to pieces, and anyone it falls on will be crushed.'

[45]When the chief priests and the Pharisees heard his parables, they knew he was talking about them. [46]They tried to arrest him, but they were afraid of the crowds, who regarded him as a prophet.

I had a dream last night, and the frustrating thing is that I can't remember what it was about. I know that when I woke up it seemed very important; indeed, so important that I wanted to write it down, but I didn't have the time. By the time I was fully awake it had gone, and I can't recall it. And yet I have known all day that it was significant, and that, if only I could get in touch with it, it might tell me something I need to know about myself or about the world.

Once upon a time there was an ancient king who posed a similar problem to his counsellors. He wanted to know what his dream meant, but he wouldn't tell them what it was. They, not being trained in modern psychology, objected strongly. Nobody has ever asked such a thing, they said. Whoever heard of such a request? If the king will only tell us his dream, then of course we will explain what it means. But the king refused – whether because he couldn't remember it, or because he was testing them, isn't quite clear. All seemed hopeless; until one wise man, getting his friends to pray for him, was granted special knowledge.

This was the king's dream. (The story is told in Daniel, chapter 2, one of many spectacular stories in that remarkable book.) He saw a huge statue: its head was made of gold, its chest and arms of silver, its middle and thighs of bronze, its legs of iron, and its feet of a mixture of iron and clay. Then there came a stone which struck the statue on its feet of iron and clay and smashed them; and the whole statue came crashing down and was broken into a million pieces. But the stone itself became a great mountain and filled the whole earth.

Once you know a bit about dreams, and about ancient theories as to what they meant – especially if it was a king dreaming them – it wouldn't be too difficult to give an interpretation. And Daniel's interpretation of the king's dream lived on in the memory of the Jews from that day to the time of Jesus and beyond. It was all about the kingdoms of the world and the **kingdom of God**.

The kingdoms of the world were the successive kingdoms of gold, silver, bronze and iron. (The king who was having the dream, conveniently enough, ruled over the golden age.) Each would be less glorious than the one before; people in those days didn't usually believe that the world was getting better, but that it was getting worse. Finally there would be a brittle kingdom, like iron mixed with clay. Then there would come something different altogether. A Stone – we'd better give it a capital letter for reasons that will soon appear – would smash the feet; in other words, it would destroy the last kingdom. The whole tottering structure of the empires of the world would come down with a crash. The Stone itself would grow to become a mountain: a new sort of kingdom, ruling the whole world in a new sort of way.

No Jew of Jesus' day would have any difficulty figuring out what it all meant for them. The kingdoms of the world, starting with Babylon and Persia, had gone on until at last it was Rome's turn. And now, surely, was the moment for the Stone to appear! The Stone, they thought, meant God's **Messiah**, who would set up the kingdom of God by destroying the world's kingdoms and starting something quite new.

What has all this to do with the **parable** of the wicked farmers killing the owner's son? Just this: Jesus, interpreting his own story, quotes from two biblical passages, Psalm 118 and Daniel 2. The stone which the builders rejected has become the top cornerstone; it wouldn't fit anywhere else in the building, but it will go in the place of greatest honour. And the stone will crush anything that collides with it. He is the Stone, the Messiah, God's anointed; he has come to bring into being the kingdom of God through which the kingdoms of the world will shiver, shake and fall to the ground.

And why is that an interpretation of the parable? Because the Stone and the Son are the same. The Son the farmers rejected is vindicated when the owner comes and destroys them, and gives the vineyard to someone else. The Stone the builders rejected is vindicated when it goes in place at the top of the corner. And – just as in English the letters of the word 'Son' are the same as the letters of the word 'Stone', with two more added, so in Hebrew, by coincidence, the letters of the word *ben* (son) are the same as those of the word *eben* (stone), with one more added.

The whole story is therefore Jesus' way of explaining what was going on then and there. It is Jesus' perspective on the very events he was involved in – rejected by those he had come to, but destined to be vindicated by God. The vineyard owner is of course God; the vineyard is Israel; the farmers are Israel's officials, and the slaves are the earlier prophets, ending with **John the Baptist**. The Son can only be Jesus himself.

It is a story full of depth, sorrow and power. It tells how he has now come to Jerusalem to confront the tenant farmers with God's demand for **repentance**, for Israel to be at last what it was called to be, the light of God's world. And it is the story of how Israel, through its official representatives, is going to refuse the demand, and will end up by killing him.

Why then the Stone? Because the last kingdom, the kingdom of iron mixed with clay, is perhaps not Rome after all. Maybe, from Jesus' point of view, it is the uneasy alliance of Herod and the chief **priests**. Maybe it is their shaky kingdom that will come crashing down when the Stone eventually falls on them. But before it can become the chief stone in the building it must first be rejected. And that, now, will not be long in coming.

MATTHEW 22.1–14

The Parable of the Wedding Feast

[1]Jesus spoke to them once again in parables.

[2]'The kingdom of heaven', he said, 'is like a king who made a wedding feast for his son. [3]He sent his slaves to call the invited guests to the wedding, and they didn't want to come.

[4]'Again he sent other slaves, with these instructions: "Say to the guests, Look! I've got my dinner ready; my bulls and fatted calves have been killed; everything is prepared. Come to the wedding!"

[5]'But they didn't take any notice. They went off, one to his own farm, another to see to his business. [6]The others laid hands on his slaves, abused them and killed them. [7](The king was angry, and sent his soldiers to destroy those murderers and burn down their city.) [8]Then he said to his slaves, "The wedding is ready, but the guests didn't deserve it. [9]So go to the roads leading out of town, and invite everyone you find to the wedding." The slaves went off into the streets and rounded up everyone they found, bad and good alike. And the wedding was filled with partygoers.

[11]'But when the king came in to look at the guests, he saw there a man who wasn't wearing a wedding suit. [12]"My friend," he said to him, "how did you get in here

without a wedding suit?" And he was speechless. [13]Then the king said to the servants, "Tie him up, hands and feet, and throw him into the darkness outside, where people weep and grind their teeth."

[14]'Many are called, you see, but few are chosen.'

'The trouble with politicians today', my friend said to me the other evening, 'is that they always tell us that if we vote for them things will get better. If only they'd tell us the truth – that the world is a dangerous place, that there are lots of wicked people trying to exploit each other, and that they will do their best to steer us through – then we might believe them.'

'Yes,' another friend chipped in, 'and that's what happens in the church as well. We are so eager to tell people that God loves them, that everything's going to be all right, that God welcomes wicked people as well as good ones – and then ordinary Christians have to live in the real world where people lie and cheat and grab what they want. Somehow it doesn't fit.'

I thought about this conversation again as I read this **parable**, which often bothers people because it doesn't say what we want it to. We want to hear a nice story about God throwing the party open to everyone. We want (as people now fashionably say) to be 'inclusive', to let everyone in. We don't want to know about judgment on the wicked, or about demanding standards of holiness, or about weeping and gnashing of teeth. Doesn't the Bible say that God will wipe away every tear from every eye?

Well, yes, it does, but you have to see that in its proper setting (Revelation 21.4, quoting Isaiah 25.8) to understand it. It doesn't mean that God will act like a soothing parent settling a child back to sleep after a nightmare. God wants us to be grown up, not babies, and part of being grown up is that we learn that actions have consequences, that moral choices matter, and that real human life isn't like a game of chess where even if we do badly the pieces get put back in the box at the end of the day and we can start again tomorrow. The great, deep mystery of God's forgiveness isn't the same as saying that whatever we do isn't really important because it'll all work out somehow.

This is not a lesson we want to learn. Often people dislike this parable because it teaches it.

Of course, when Jesus told the parable it had a particular point and focus. (It's possible that verse 7, the bit in brackets, was added later, perhaps by Matthew himself, so that his readers would make the connection between what Jesus was saying and the terrible events of AD 70. We shall see more about this when we get to chapter 24.) The parable follows straight on from the devastating story of the wicked tenant farmers in chapter 21, and rams the point home. Everyone would know what a story about a landowner with a vineyard was referring to; equally everyone in Jesus' day would know the point of a story about a king throwing a wedding party for his son. (Jesus may well have told this kind of story several times; there's a quite different version of it in Luke 14.15–24.) This story is about the coming of God's **kingdom**, and in particular the arrival of the **Messiah**.

Israel's leaders in Jesus' day, and the many people who followed them, were like guests invited to a wedding – God's wedding party, the party he was throwing for his son. But they had refused. Galilee had refused, for the most part; think back to Jesus' sad warnings in 11.20–24. Now Jerusalem was refusing the invitation as well. God was planning the great party for which they had waited so long. The Messiah was here, and they didn't want to know. They abused and killed the prophets who had tried to tell them about it, and the result was that their city would be destroyed.

But now for the **good news** – though it wasn't good news for the people who were originally invited. God was sending

83

out new messengers, to the wrong parts of town, to tell every-one and anyone to come to the party. And they came in droves. We don't have to look far in Matthew's **gospel** to see who they were. The tax-collectors, the prostitutes, the riff-raff, the nobodies, the blind and lame, the people who thought they'd been forgotten. They were thrilled that God's **message** was for them after all.

But there was a difference between this wide-open invitation and the message so many want to hear today. We want to hear that everyone is all right exactly as they are; that God loves us as we are and doesn't want us to change. People often say this when they want to justify particular types of behaviour, but the argument doesn't work. When the blind and lame came to Jesus, he didn't say, 'You're all right as you are'. He healed them. They wouldn't have been satisfied with anything less. When the prostitutes and extortioners came to Jesus (or, for that matter, to **John the Baptist**), he didn't say, 'You're all right as you are'. His love reached them *where* they were, but his love refused to let them stay *as* they were. Love wants the best for the beloved. Their lives were transformed, healed, changed.

Actually, nobody really believes that God wants *everyone* to stay exactly as they are. God loves serial killers and child-molesters; God loves ruthless and arrogant businessmen; God loves manipulative mothers who damage their children's emotions for life. But the point of God's love is that he wants them to change. He hates what they're doing and the effect it has on everyone else – and on themselves, too. Ultimately, if he's a good God, he cannot allow that sort of behaviour, and that sort of person, if they don't change, to remain for ever in the party he's throwing for his son.

That is the point of the end of the story, which is otherwise very puzzling. Of course, within the story itself it sounds quite arbitrary. Where did all these other guests get their wedding costumes from? If the servants just herded them in, how did they have time to change their clothes? Why should this one man be thrown out because he didn't have the right thing to wear? Isn't that just the sort of social exclusion that the gospel rejects?

Well, yes, of course, at that level. But that's not how parables work. The point of the story is that Jesus is telling the truth, the truth that political and religious leaders often like to hide: the truth that God's kingdom is a kingdom in which love and justice and truth and mercy and holiness reign unhindered. They are the clothes you need to wear for the wedding. And if you refuse to put them on, you are saying you don't want to stay at the party. That is the reality. If we don't have the courage to say so, we are deceiving ourselves, and everyone who listens to us.

MATTHEW 22.15–22

Paying Taxes to Caesar

[15]Then the Pharisees went and plotted how they might trap him into saying the wrong thing. [16]They sent their followers to him, with the Herodians.

'Teacher,' they said, 'we know that you are truthful, and that you teach God's way truthfully. You don't care what anyone thinks about you, because you don't try to flatter people or favour them. [17]So tell us what you think. Is it lawful to pay tribute to Caesar, or not?'

[18]Jesus knew their evil intentions.

'Why are you trying to trick me, you hypocrites?' he said. [19]'Show me the tribute coin.' They brought him a dinar.

[20]'This . . . image,' said Jesus, 'and this . . . inscription. Who do they belong to?'

[21]'Caesar,' they said.

'Well then,' said Jesus, 'you'd better give Caesar what belongs to Caesar! And – give God what belongs to God!'

[22] When they heard that they were astonished. They left him and went away.

It was election time. The politicians were out campaigning. The journalists were everywhere, interviewing people, taking photographs, setting up debates. Radio and television seemed full of it all.

But this time round everyone seemed jumpy. Politicians used to be only too eager to be on television; now they realized that the broadcasters could be out to get them. Things came to a head when one leading politician realized that what looked like an ordinary studio audience had actually been filled with people waiting to ask trick questions, to make him look stupid, to attack and vilify him rather than trying to find out what was really going on. The broadcasters, of course, protested that these were just ordinary people voicing their concerns . . . and before long everyone was talking about the programme rather than the politics. This was, of course, what the broadcasters (with an eye to their advertising revenue) had been hoping for.

Trick questions that put people on the spot have been around as long as there have been public issues and leaders offering new programmes. This one, which the **Pharisees** put to Jesus, had an obvious double edge. The issue of paying tax to the Roman emperor was one of the hottest topics in the Middle East in Jesus' day. Imagine how you'd like it if you woke up one morning and discovered that people from the other end of the world had marched in to your country and demanded that you pay them tax as the reward for having your land stolen! That sort of thing still causes riots and revolutions, and it had done just that when Jesus was growing up in Galilee.

One of the most famous Jewish leaders when Jesus was a boy, a man called Judas (a good revolutionary name in the

Jewish world), had led a revolt precisely on this issue. The Romans had crushed it mercilessly, leaving crosses around the countryside, with dead and dying revolutionaries on them, as a warning that paying the tax was compulsory, not optional. The Pharisees' question came, as we would say, with a health warning. Tell people they shouldn't pay, and you might end up on a cross.

At the same time, of course, anyone leading a **kingdom-of-God** movement would be expected to oppose the tax, or face the ridicule and resentment of the people. Surely the whole point of God becoming king was that Caesar wouldn't be? If Jesus wasn't intending to get rid of the tax and all that it meant, what had they followed him from Galilee for? Why had they all shouted Hosanna a few days earlier? If Jesus had been a politician on a television programme, you can imagine the audience's delight, and the producer's glee, when someone asked this question. This one will really give him a hard time.

Before Jesus answers, he asks them for a coin. Or rather, asking them for a coin is really the beginning of his answer, the start of a strategic outflanking move. When they produce the coin, the dinar that was used to pay the tax, they are showing that they themselves are handling the hated currency.

Among the reasons it was hated was what was on the coin. Jews weren't allowed to put images of people, human faces, on their coins; but Caesar, of course, had his image stamped on his. And around the edge of the coin, proclaiming to all the world who he was, Caesar had words that would send a shudder through any loyal or devout Jew. '**Son of God** . . . high **priest**' – was that who Caesar thought he was? How could any Jew be happy to handle stuff like that?

We watch the scene as Jesus takes the coin from them, like someone being handed a dead rat. He looks at it with utter distaste. 'Whose is this . . . *image*? And who is it who gives himself an *inscription* like that?' He's already shown what he thinks of Caesar, but he hasn't said anything that could get him into trouble. He has turned the question around, and is ready to throw it back at them.

'It's Caesar's,' they reply, stating the obvious, but admitting that they themselves carry Caesar's coinage.

'Well then,' says Jesus, 'you'd better pay Caesar back in his own coin, hadn't you?' Astonishment. What did he mean? 'Paying Caesar back in his own coin' sounded like revolution; but standing there with the coin in his hand it sounded as though he was saying you should pay the tax . . .

'. . . and you'd better pay God back in his own coin, too!' More astonishment. Did he mean that the kingdom of God *was* more important than the kingdom of Caesar, after all? Or what?

Let's be clear. Jesus wasn't trying to give an answer, for all time, on the relationship between God and political authority. That wasn't the point. He was countering the Pharisees' challenge to him with a sharp challenge in return. Was it, after all, they who were compromised? Had they really given full allegiance to their God? Were they themselves playing games, keeping Caesar happy while speaking of God?

We can only fully understand what Jesus was doing when we see his answer in the light of the whole story. Jesus knew – he had already told the **disciples** – that he was himself going to be crucified, to share the fate of the tax-rebels of his boyhood. He wasn't trying to wriggle out of personal or political danger. He was continuing to walk straight towards it. But he was doing so on his own terms. His vocation was not to be the sort of revolutionary they had known. The kingdom of God would defeat the kingdom of Caesar, not by conventional means, but by the victory of God's love and power over the even greater empire of death itself. And that's what the next story is all about.

MATTHEW 22.23–33

The Question of the Resurrection

²³The same day some Sadducees came to him. (The Sadducees deny the resurrection.) Their question was this.

²⁴'Teacher,' they began, 'Moses said, "If a man dies without children, his brother should marry his widow and raise up seed for his brother." ²⁵Well now, there were seven brothers living among us. The first got married, and then died, and since he didn't have children he left his wife to his brother. ²⁶The same thing happened with the second and the third, and so on with all seven. ²⁷Last of all the woman died. ²⁸So: in the resurrection, whose wife will she be, of all the seven? All of them had married her, after all.'

²⁹This was Jesus' answer to them:

'You are quite mistaken,' he said, 'because you don't know your Bibles or God's power. ³⁰In the resurrection, you see, people don't marry or get married off; they are like angels in heaven. ³¹But as for the resurrection of the dead, did you never read what was said to you by God, in these words: "I am the God of Abraham, and the God of Isaac, and the God of Jacob?" He isn't God of the dead, but of the living.'

³³The crowds heard this, and they were astonished at his teaching.

I once sat on a college committee where two older members had a regular tactic for stopping any change that might have been proposed. When one of the younger members (myself, for instance) proposed doing something that would really benefit the whole community (well, I would say that, wouldn't I), one of these two could be relied upon to come up with a ridiculous story of what might conceivably happen if we did such a thing.

On one occasion, for instance, someone had proposed that by the entrance to the college there should be a system of mailboxes so that every member of the college could collect his or her mail easily from the right box, rather than having, as we then did, a small number of boxes with a large number of letters stuffed into each. Many other colleges had sensible systems; why couldn't we?

Straight away one of the blockers went into action. 'Ah, but', he said, 'supposing you put in these new mailboxes; they'll probably have to go right down to floor level. Then supposing somebody comes by with a dog. And supposing the dog decides to lift its hind leg right beside the mailboxes. You wouldn't like that to happen to your mail, would you?' The picture was so silly it was actually funny; but by the time everyone had laughed, the nonsensical story had had its effect. Half the room had come to believe, without any actual argument, that there were serious problems about the proposal.

We know from several sources that the **Sadducees** – the let's-keep-things-as-they-are party within the Judaism of Jesus' day – were good at telling silly stories to make the idea of **resurrection** look stupid and unbelievable. The story they told here is a typical folktale, with the seven brothers like the seven dwarfs in the Snow White story, or the heroes in *The Magnificent Seven*. Its purpose is simply to set out a highly unlikely situation to force the issue.

What is really important here is why the Sadducees were so keen to rubbish the idea of resurrection in the first place. The answer is that they knew it was a revolutionary doctrine; and they, as the people in power, were keen to stop it if they could. Actually, they couldn't stop it. Most people of Jesus' day believed what the **Pharisees** said, that God would raise them to new life when he finally brought in the New Age that everyone was longing for. But this story reminds us of the lengths to which people will go to defend a position which has social and theological elements woven tightly together.

There are several things going on all together, both in the story the Sadducees tell and in the reply Jesus gives.

First, they quote what is to us a rather strange biblical law (Deuteronomy 25.5): that if a married man dies childless, his brother must marry the widow, and the children of the new marriage will count as the heirs of the dead man. This law was vital for the people of God BC, to whom God had made promises about the continuance of their 'seed' or 'family'. ('Seed' in verse 24 means 'family' or 'descendants'.) So far as possible, the people were to prevent family lines and tribal identity dying out in Israel. This was one way of doing so.

But Jesus has come, it seems, to bring about God's renewal of his people. They will now be a worldwide family, marked not by ethnic origin or tribal identity but by the new creation of the **gospel**. The old laws designed to keep the family going will be irrelevant. That's the first reason for rejecting their story.

Second, when God raises people to new life they will have passed into a new world order in which death itself has been left behind. (Otherwise, resurrection would simply collapse into reincarnation, an endless cycle of death and rebirth.) But this will mean a whole new *kind* of life, which at present we can only guess at. Our present bodies are decaying all the time; it's very hard to think what a non-decaying body would be like. (Paul faces the same question in 1 Corinthians 15.) Similarly, there will be no need to propagate the species, and hence no need for sexual activity. Again, most humans find it very hard to think of a non-sexual world, but that's what Jesus probably means when he says that resurrected people will be 'like angels'. (If you grumble that this makes God a killjoy, remember what C. S. Lewis said: asking if there will be sexual activity in the future world is like the child who, on being told that sex was the greatest pleasure known to humans, assumed that people ate chocolates at the same time.)

In particular, third, what the Sadducees were missing was any real engagement with the meaning of the Bible, and any real awareness of just how great and powerful the creator God is. They claimed to base themselves on the books of Moses (the first five books of the Bible), but they had missed the real thrust of the whole thing. Israel's God was and is the creator of the world, who is content to describe himself as the God of Abraham, Isaac and Jacob even though they died long ago. He is holding them in life still, and one day they will be raised, along with all God's people, past, present and future, to enjoy the new world that God will make.

The great thing about this belief, as the Pharisees and Sadducees both knew, is that people who believe it become more ready to work for God in the present time, more eager to see God's promises of justice, peace and new life begin to take effect in today's world. The revolution which Jesus had hinted at in the discussion about paying tax to Caesar was the revolution of God's **kingdom** in which all the kingdoms of the world, which rely on the power of death to keep them in place, will be swept away before the deathless life and power of God's New Age.

MATTHEW 22.34–46

The Great Commandment, and David's Master

³⁴When the Pharisees heard that Jesus had silenced the Sadducees, they got together in a group. ³⁵One of them, a lawyer, put him on the spot with this question.

³⁶'Teacher,' he said, 'which is the most important commandment in the law?'

³⁷'You must love the Lord your God', replied Jesus, 'with all your heart, with all your life, and with all your strength. ³⁸This is the first commandment, and it's the one that really matters. ³⁹The second is similar, and it's this: You must love your neighbour as yourself. ⁴⁰The entire law consists of footnotes to these two commandments – and that goes for the prophets, too.'

⁴¹While the Pharisees were gathered there, Jesus asked them,

> [42] 'What's your view of the Messiah? Whose son is he?'
>
> 'David's', they said to him.
>
> [43] 'So how then', said Jesus, 'can David (speaking by the spirit) call him "Master", when he says,
>
> > [44] The Master says to my Master,
> > Sit here at my right hand,
> > Until I place your enemies
> > Down beneath your feet.
>
> [45] 'If David calls him "Master", how can he be his son?'
>
> [46] Nobody was able to answer him a single word. From that day on nobody dared ask him anything.

I watched on television a tennis match between two of the game's finest players. Both had been playing well, but towards the end one of them seemed to rise to new heights. The match ended with two stunning games, when the winner not only did everything right but superlatively. First his opponent served, and each serve was met with a return that won the point. Then, when it was his turn to serve, each one was a clean ace. Game, set and match.

That's how the end of Matthew 22 is meant to strike us. The answer the opponents couldn't question was followed by the question they couldn't answer. Which is the greatest commandment, they asked? Jesus' answer was so traditional that nobody could challenge him on it, and so deeply searching that everyone else would be challenged by it. Then it was Jesus' turn: is the **Messiah** David's son or David's Master – or perhaps both? They'd never asked that question before, and they certainly didn't know the answer, even though it was standing in front of them in flesh and blood.

The next occasions when Jesus will meet his opponents will be in the garden when they arrest him, in the Council when they accuse him, and on the cross when they mock him. But each time they will know, he will know, and we as Matthew's readers will know, that he knows the answers to these questions and they do not. He also knows, and Matthew wants us to know as well, that his arrest, trial and crucifixion are precisely the way in which Jesus is fulfilling the two great commandments, and the way in which he is being enthroned both as David's son, the true king of Israel, and David's master, David's Lord. This is how, as the **son of God** in a still fuller sense, he has come to rescue his people. Unless we are prepared to see these questions in this light we will remain shallow in our understanding of them.

Let's deal with the surface level, though, because that matters greatly as well. Many Jewish teachers posed the question as to which was the greatest out of all the 613 commandments in the **law** of Moses. Many would have agreed substantially with the answer that Jesus gave. Equally important, though, these commandments were not simply among the things the Jews were supposed to *do*. They formed part of the *prayer* that every devout Jew prayed every day, in a tradition that continues unbroken to the present time.

But did people actually keep these commandments? Jesus has already spoken, in chapter 15, of the need for the heart to be renewed so that people will produce words and deeds which are appropriate, rather than making them impure. His challenge in the Sermon on the Mount was that the heart should be renewed, not just that the outward actions should conform with the proper standard.

But how could this be done? Even those of us who have spent our whole lives trying to follow Jesus and live by his grace and love know that the heart doesn't seem to get renewed all in one go. Many, many bits of darkness and impurity still lurk in its depths, and sometimes take a lot of work, prayer and counsel to dig out and replace with the love which we all agree should really be there.

Once more, what Jesus says here about loving God, and loving one another, only makes sense when we set it within Matthew's larger **gospel** picture, of Jesus dying for the sins of the world, and rising again with the **message** of new life. That's when these commandments begin to come into their own: when they are seen not as orders to be obeyed in our own strength, but as invitations and promises to a new way of life in which, bit by bit, hatred and pride can be left behind and love can become a reality.

Something similar is going on with Jesus' remarkable explanation about who the Messiah really is. Matthew is quite clear, of course, that Jesus is indeed the **son of David** (1.1; 20.30; etc.). The point is that simply calling him that doesn't tell the whole story. By itself, 'son of David' could mean, and for many Jews of the time did mean, the coming king who would win military victories over Israel's enemies. Such a figure would hardly encourage people to love God with all their hearts and their neighbours as themselves, especially when we realize, as the Sermon on the Mount insists, that when we say the word 'God' we mean the creator and lover of the whole world, not just of one segment within it.

But if this God himself were to become human, as Matthew has insisted is the case (1.23), then we would be faced with a very different situation. If David's son is also David's master, then the warlike Davidic Messiah of popular Jewish imagination will be, after all, one who will bring the saving, healing rule of this creator God to the whole world. And the 'enemies' that he will put 'under his feet', as Psalm 110 insists, will not be the nationalist enemies of an ethnic 'people of God', but the ultimate enemies of the whole human race, and indeed of the whole world; in other words, sin itself, and death, which it brings.

It is because Jesus sees that sin and death are still at work, in the Israel which prides itself on its special status, that he opposes so vehemently any attempt to prop up that national standing. That is why he will now launch into a full-scale denunciation of the attempts that were being made to do just that. But it is because Jesus knows that sin and death can only be defeated by David's master going to meet them in single, unarmed combat that he continues his work, as Matthew will tell us, all the way to the cross itself.

MATTHEW 23.1–12

Warnings against Scribes and Pharisees

[1]Then Jesus spoke to the crowds and to his disciples:

[2]'The scribes and Pharisees', he said, 'sit on the seat of Moses. [3]So you must do whatever they tell you, and keep it, but don't do the things they do. You see, they *talk* but they don't *do*. [4]They tie up heavy bundles which are difficult to carry, and they dump them on people's shoulders – but they themselves aren't prepared to lift a little finger to move them!

[5]'Everything they do is for show, to be seen by people. Yes, they make their prayer-boxes large and their prayer-tassels long, [6]and they love the chief places at dinners, the main seats in the synagogues, [7]the greetings in the marketplaces, and having people call them "Rabbi".

[8]'You mustn't be called "Rabbi". You have one teacher, and you are all one family. [9]And you shouldn't call anyone "father" on earth, because you have one father, in heaven. [10]Nor should you be called "teacher", because you have one teacher, the Messiah.

[11]'The greatest among you should be your servant. [12]People who make themselves great will be humbled; and people who humble themselves will become great.'

The man in the camping shop was good at his job.

'This is the kind of tent you'll need,' he said. 'It'll last through all weathers, enough room for all your kit, easy to put up.'

Gratefully, I added it to the pile of maps, socks and waterproof clothing. Then it was time for boots.

'These are the best there are,' he said. 'Solid sole, dependable uppers, support for the ankles, walk through mud or grass or pebbles or hard rock. Just the job.'

I agreed. Then we came to cooking equipment. Again he knew just what I needed: the stove, the fuel, the storage boxes. And the same with the food itself: packs of long-lasting but nourishing food and drink. I'd have to get water from day to day (or refill the bottles from mountain streams), but here were a couple of bottles to start me off.

Then it was a sleeping bag, then it was something to burn to keep insects away, then it was a torch and an emergency first aid kit. And so on.

Finally it was the pack. 'This should be big enough,' he said, lifting down a simply enormous haversack. 'And it's waterproof, too, and, yes, sits nicely on the shoulders, that one.'

As I paid the bill, his assistant kindly and carefully placed all the items into the pack itself. It rested, invitingly, on the counter beside the till, full of my new holiday lifestyle.

I tried to pick it up and swing it round onto my back, casually, as though I did this sort of thing every day. An awkward moment. I changed my mind and turned round, away from the counter, bent my knees a little to get to the right level, and inched backwards towards the huge pack. The assistant helped me get my arms into the straps. I straightened my knees and smiled bravely, wondering if I would get out of the shop, let alone a hundred miles through the mountains.

'What sort of vacations do *you* have, then?' I asked the expert salesman.

'Oh, I just go to the seaside,' he said. 'Bad back. Can't carry stuff like that.'

By the time I reached the end of the street I was thinking of the **scribes** and **Pharisees**.

With this chapter we are launched into the last of the five great blocks of teaching which Matthew has constructed as the backbone (so to speak) of his **gospel**. The Sermon on the Mount came first in chapters 5–7. Then the commissioning of the **disciples** in chapter 10. Then the **parables** of the **kingdom** in chapter 13. Then the material on living as a community in obedience to Jesus' teaching, in chapter 18. And now another long, final block of teaching, balancing the Sermon on the Mount; chapters 23–25, looking ahead to the future and warning of what is to come.

In all of this, Matthew is saying, we are to regard Jesus as being like Moses, only more so. Moses (they believed) gave the people the five books of the **law**; Jesus gives them the five books of the new **covenant**, the new relationship between God and the world. Moses brought the people through the desert and led them to the point where they were ready to cross over the Jordan and go into the promised land. Jesus is leading his people through the desert to the point where he will lead them through death itself and on into the new world which God is going to make. Only, unlike Moses, he won't stay on this side of the river, leaving someone else to take the people across. He will go on ahead, like his namesake Joshua, and lead them himself into the new world.

And now he finds himself surrounded with people who are telling their fellow Jews about the heavy packs they need to carry on their backs for the journey – but who never dream of carrying such things themselves. The **legal experts** who are always going on about Moses: Moses said this, Moses said that, do this, don't do that, watch out for this danger, remember to do this every day, and so on and so on. From one point of view it looks like wonderful devotion, a lavish attention to the detail of the commandments which God gave to Israel. But from another point of view it looks like a salesman telling a hiker all the things he should carry, but never venturing out for a walk himself.

Jesus' charge against the scribes and Pharisees, which builds up through this chapter as a devastating catalogue of indictments, is not that they were wrong to pay attention to Moses. Matthew has made it clear all along (e.g. 5.17–19) that the Mosaic law, the **Torah**, was good and God-given. It should indeed be observed. But what really mattered in it, as he said in 22.37–39, were the big central matters, loving God and loving your neighbour, which means justice and mercy and faithfulness (23.23). When it came to those, he declared, the legal experts who were so good at telling other people what to do never lifted a finger to move the really heavy burdens.

Instead, they concentrated on outward show. Large prayer-cases (known as 'phylacteries', leather bands and cases containing prayers, worn on the arm and the head) could easily be seen by others, and noted as a sign of piety. Long prayer-tassels at the four corners of the outer garment showed, again, how scrupulous the wearer wanted to be thought. Titles of honour, places of honour: all the fame that a small society can afford. Jesus throws it all to the winds. It shows they haven't understood what Moses was on about.

Generations of preachers have used this passage to criticize church leaders who like dressing up and being seen in public. That's fair enough. But we shouldn't forget that the scribes and Pharisees were not simply what we would call 'religious' leaders. They were, just as much, what we would call social and political leaders, or at least the leaders of popular parties and pressure groups.

What are today's equivalents? Some might be the leaders, whether elected or unelected, in our wider societies, who give themselves airs on the media, who rejoice in their 'celebrity' status, who make grand pronouncements about public values while running lucrative but shady businesses on the side, who use their position to gain influence for their families and friends, and who allow their private interests secretly to determine the public policy of their country. Before we indulge, as Christians, in inward-looking polemic against other members of our own family of **faith**, let's be clear that the problem Jesus identified is not confined to churches, but runs through most modern societies from top to bottom.

When we've got that clear, then of course there are several lessons for every church and Christian group to learn. It's not just about the titles we use for our teachers and leaders. The New Testament gives us a variety of those (e.g. Ephesians 4.11). It's about the attitudes that go with them, which can be just as bad when people avoid official titles as when they use them. What matters is the huge and humbling principle of verses 11 and 12.

When we look at those verses we realize, not for the first or last time, that we are indeed called to follow Jesus himself, who issued these denunciations not from a great or pompous height, but on the way to the cross. He had seen that on the journey he and his true followers had to make there would be no room for inflated luggage. He had already promised that his load was easy and his burden was light, and that people carrying heavy loads should take his instead (11.28–30). Now he was on the way to shoulder the heaviest burden of all, so that his people would never again have to be weighed down by it.

MATTHEW 23.13–22

Condemnation of Scribes and Pharisees (1)

[13]'Woe betide you, scribes and Pharisees, you hypocrites!' Jesus continued. 'You lock up the kingdom of heaven in front of people's faces. You don't go in yourselves, and you stop other people who might have gone in from doing so.

¹⁵'Woe betide you, scribes and Pharisees, you hypocrites! You cross sea and land to make one single Gentile take up Judaism, and when that happens you make the convert twice as much a child of Gehenna as you are yourselves.

¹⁶'Woe betide you, you blind guides! This is what you say: "If anyone swears by the Temple, it's nothing; but if anyone swears by the gold in the Temple, the oath is valid." ¹⁷How crazy and blind can you get! Which is greater, the gold, or the Temple that makes the gold sacred? ¹⁸And you say, "If anyone swears by the altar, it's nothing; but if anyone swears by the gift on it, the oath is valid." ¹⁹How blind you are! Which is greater, the gift, or the altar that makes the gift sacred? ²⁰So whoever swears by the altar swears by it and by everything on it. ²¹And whoever swears by the Temple swears by it and by the one who lives in it. ²²And whoever swears by heaven swears by the throne of God and by the one who sits on it.'

I once preached a sermon in a church in America. I spoke particularly of the way in which the ancient pagan gods and goddesses were starting to infiltrate our culture once more, and how as Christians we should learn to recognize the insidious ways in which this happens.

I stood shaking hands at the door. One lady of a certain age walked up to me, looking delighted.

'By Jove,' she said, 'that was a fine sermon.'

The look on my face made her realize what she had said. Obviously Jove has never been a major deity in America, but the only reason for invoking the name is that he once was elsewhere. When Jesus declares that our careless words will reveal who we really are, it is perhaps time to examine some things we say without even thinking about it.

'Cross my heart and hope to die.' 'I swear on the Holy Bible.' 'Upon my honour.' I used to hear these all the time when I was younger. 'I swear on the heads of my children.' 'By my mother's grave.' I've heard those quite often, more recently. No doubt everybody could add their own. Why do we *do* it?

Is it just insecurity? If we're not sure that our words will carry sufficient weight by themselves, why do we add these pointless extras? Is it an attempt to stiffen the backbone of our sentences? If so, it's self-defeating. You might as well try to prop up a sagging tree with a wet towel. What begins as a sign of insecurity, or an attempt to make our speech a bit more colourful without the effort of actual thought, continues as a habit, and eventually becomes mere noise that we're hardly aware of. Jesus' saying about being judged by our careless words comes home to roost (12.36).

It is interesting to note that Jesus warns, among other things, against swearing by **heaven**. In Western culture at least, and within Western churches, saying 'Heavens!' or some equivalent has long been acceptable in polite society, whereas saying 'Hell!' has not. It's a measure of how far we've allowed social customs to dominate us, rather than Jesus' commands: he prohibits swearing by heaven, but never mentions swearing by **hell**.

Presumably he would rather we did neither, and that is of course the point of the passage in the Sermon on the Mount about swearing (5.33–37). In fact, the present passage goes deeper than that question, and addresses the question of the attitudes to the **Temple** that show up in the **scribes'** and **Pharisees'** decisions about which oaths will count and which won't.

Basically, he accuses them of getting things the wrong way round. They are valuing the gold above the Temple, and the gift above the altar. They are placing higher worth on the objects that human beings have brought into God's presence than on God's presence itself. But if the gold and the gifts mean anything, it's because the Temple and the altar mean something. And they mean what they mean because of God's promise to be present there. In other words, the teachers are taking God's name in vain. They are guilty of breaking the third commandment. And they are covering it up with slick arguments about what counts and what doesn't.

All of this results in the teachers in question being twice condemned as 'blind' (verses 16, 19). They can't see what's really important, or rather *who* is really important. They are like someone who has never learned to read trying to settle a dispute on the respective merits of Shakespeare and Goethe. They show by their every ruling that they simply don't know what they're talking about.

The other short passages at the start of this section put the spotlight on what happens to other people as a result of the activity of the scribes and Pharisees. Their complex legal systems lead them not only to devote their own lives to details which have nothing to do with the real purpose of the **law**, but also to make it impossible for serious seekers after truth, or after God, to find the way. And when they expend every effort to find non-Jews who express interest in their way of life, they impose such burdens on them that they are worse off than if they'd never heard of Judaism in the first place.

It's important at this stage to say something about who these people were whom Jesus is attacking in these passages. One sometimes hears it said that they represent 'the Jews'. It's true that Matthew's **gospel**, not least this chapter, has sometimes been used as a weapon in anti-Jewish, or even anti-Semitic, propaganda. But that is a flagrant misuse of this text. In Jesus' day, and on to our own day, the great majority of Jews have been, to put it crudely, neither scribes nor Pharisees.

True, the Pharisees' laws and regulations were developed after AD 70 by the **rabbis**, who became the dominant factor within Judaism and remain so to this day. But Jesus' criticisms were primarily against those of his own time who, he could see, were leading Israel astray, causing Israel to look in the wrong direction, at the very moment when its hour, and indeed its **Messiah**, had come. The main reason he is taking the trouble to denounce them in such detail is because they are distracting attention at the crucial moment. Their particular failings are simply extra evidence that they are not in fact the true guides that Israel needs at this fateful moment in its history.

Equally, some have supposed that Jesus, whom we think of as kindly and loving, could never have denounced anyone, least of all his fellow-Jews, in such sharp tones. It has sometimes been suggested that these sayings belong to a later age, when divisions emerged between 'official' Christianity and Judaism. But that is unnecessary. Jesus was aware throughout his public career of fierce opposition from parties in Judaism with rival agendas. The present chapter consists, in fact, of a solemn, almost ritual, denunciation of them for their hollow piety and misguided teaching.

Anyone who supposes, however, that these failings were, or are, confined to one religion, culture, or group should look at their own society, and (alas) at their own church, and think again. There is much to learn historically from studying these sayings. But there is also much to take seriously as we look around us at today's guides and leaders and ask what Jesus might have said to them.

MATTHEW 23.23–33

Condemnation of Scribes and Pharisees (2)

[23]'Woe betide you, scribes and Pharisees, you hypocrites!' Jesus went on. 'You tithe mint and dill and cummin, and you omit the serious matters of the law like justice, mercy and loyalty. You should have done these, without neglecting the others. [24]You're blind guides! You filter out a gnat, but you gulp down a camel!

[25]'Woe betide you, scribes and Pharisees, you hypocrites! You scrub the outside of the cup and the dish, but the inside is full of extortion and moral flabbiness. [26]You blind Pharisee, first make the inside of the cup clean, and then the outside will be clean as well.

[27]'Woe betide you, scribes and Pharisees, you hypocrites!

You're like whitewashed graves, which look very fine on the outside, but inside they are full of the bones of the dead and uncleanness of every kind. [28]That's like you: on the outside you appear to be virtuous and law-abiding, but inside you are full of hypocrisy and lawlessness.

[29]'Woe betide you, scribes and Pharisees, you hypocrites! You build the tombs of the prophets, and you decorate the memorials of the righteous, [30]and you say, "If we'd lived in the days of our ancestors, we wouldn't have gone along with them in killing the prophets." [31]So you testify against yourselves that you are the children of the people who murdered the prophets! [32]Well then, go ahead: complete the work your ancestors began! [33]You snakes, you nest of vipers, how can you escape the judgment of Gehenna?'

We arrived at the cottage shortly before dark. It had been a lovely sunny day, and now the light was fading through the tall trees at the far end of the garden. The cottage looked, in this light, like a dream. A blackbird was sitting on its thatched roof. A wisp of smoke arose from the chimney, giving a faint smell of a log fire. A light twinkled from an old leaded window. The old stone walls glowed in the pink evening light.

We went inside. The shock was almost unbearable. Old newspapers covered the floor. What was left of the carpet was dirty, and the mice had obviously been nibbling it. Two of the doors were swinging loose, their hinges half broken. Milk bottles, full of rancid, solid milk sat untouched by the kitchen door. A dripping noise came from somewhere round the back where a pipe had burst and never been fixed. The light that had twinkled through the window was a single naked bulb hanging in the middle of the front room. And the wood burning in the fireplace was not a stack of logs cut from an old tree, but the broken limbs of chairs which had been chopped up for firewood. It was a human tragedy, but from the outside we would never have known.

In a dream, say the psychiatrists, a house represents yourself. Maybe that's why the horror of that experience was so powerful. We identify with houses. Their tidiness, or perhaps cheerful clutter, reflect the type of people we are. Their colour schemes speak volumes about the taste of the owner. Their whole 'feel' and flavour conveys the mood of the people who have lived there. 'Houses live and die', wrote T. S. Eliot in *Four Quartets*. And when they die, often they die from the inside first.

The centre of Jesus' accusation against the **Pharisees** of his day was that they were like that sad and terrible house. Outwardly they were fine. Those who passed them in the street were impressed. Those who saw their scrupulous observance of the **law** regarded them as virtuous, as excellent Jews, as people with whom God was surely pleased.

But go through the front door and see what you find. Extortion and moral flabbiness, says Jesus (verse 25); the second phrase literally means 'weakness of will', 'self-indulgence'. It's the term philosophers used when they faced the puzzle of people who knew what they ought to do and then failed to do it. For the **scribes** and Pharisees this was even worse. They knew what to do because it was in God's law. They were themselves teachers of that law; and yet they didn't do it.

It perhaps needs to be said that from all our evidence of first-century Jewish teachers we know that there were plenty of them who wouldn't have fitted this description. St Paul had been a leading Pharisee, and by his own account (when he had nothing to gain from it) he was a very successful one (Philippians 3.4–6). There were great leaders like Gamaliel, whom Luke clearly regards as a fine teacher (Acts 5.33–39). There were noble sages like Rabbi Akiba, who went on praying the *Shema* prayer ('Hear, O Israel: YHWH our God, YHWH is one') as the Romans tortured him to death in AD 135. There were saints in that tradition, all right.

But we have every reason to suppose that there were many,

probably the majority, who went along for the ride, or more particularly for the *political* agenda that the Pharisees adopted. They liked the idea of being rigorous about the **Torah** because it suited their nationalist ambitions. But when it came to the actual spiritual and moral struggle to make the inside of the house match the outside, they hadn't even begun.

Once again, this whole attack on the Pharisees only makes sense within the larger picture which Matthew is drawing. Jesus is on his way to accomplish the real **covenant** renewal (see 26.28) which all the Pharisees' intensification of Torah could not achieve. He was on his way to draw on to himself all the wickedness of the world, including for that matter the wickednesses he was denouncing in this chapter and elsewhere; to take their full force on to himself and so to exhaust it. It would be a bad mistake, then, to read a chapter like this as simply a moral denunciation. It would be still worse to read it as a moral denunciation *of somebody else*. That's halfway to committing the very mistake that's being attacked.

Having said that, we shouldn't miss the note which emerges at the end, and points to what is to follow. Jesus sees the present self-styled teachers of the law as fitting in exactly to the pattern of previous generations: killing the prophets and truly righteous people of old. Though they protest that they would not have done such a thing, Jesus knows from their longstanding opposition to him that their protests are only skin deep. They are true children of their prophet-killing ancestors, and are about to complete the work by handing over to death the greatest prophet of them all.

MATTHEW 23.34–39

Judgment on Jerusalem and Its Leaders

³⁴'Because of all this,' Jesus concluded, 'I'm sending you prophets, wise and learned people. Some of them you will kill

and crucify. Some of them you will whip in your synagogues. You'll chase them from town to town. [35]That's how all the righteous blood that's been shed on earth, from the blood of righteous Abel to the blood of Zechariah son of Barachiah (you murdered him between sanctuary and altar) – all that blood will come upon you. [36]I'm telling you the solemn truth: it will all come on this generation.

[37]'Jerusalem, Jerusalem, killing the prophets and stoning those who are sent to you! How often have I longed to gather up your children, the way a hen gathers up her brood under her wings, and you didn't want me to! [38]Now, see here: your house has been abandoned by God; it's a ruin. [39]Yes, I tell you: you won't see me again from now on until you say, "Welcome in the name of the Lord!"'

For many city-dwellers, myself included, life on a farm can appear idyllic. Memories of brief visits to farming relatives when I was a child combine with the view of peaceful rural life seen from a car or a train. Living in close touch with the land, with seedtime and harvest, with animals – this seems just what we want as an antidote to the concrete jungle, the frantic pace of life, the industrial pollution that is a daily reality for most of us.

But any farm-dweller will tell you that the reality is very different. Farming means relentless hard work under difficult conditions. And there are just as many dangers and hazards on a farm as in a town. Fire on a farm, in particular, is a nightmare. The smell of burning flesh is sickening. Animals themselves have a deep instinctive sense of danger and fear, and there are many farmyards today where dogs and cats, geese and chickens, and other small or domestic animals, are suffering traumas and don't know why.

One of Jesus' most vivid illustrations concerns the hen and the chickens caught in a farmyard fire. Throughout the animal world, of course, the behaviour of mothers whose young are threatened is remarkable. But in this case there is a specially interesting phenomenon. There have been recorded instances of a mother hen, faced with a fire, collecting her young chickens under her wings to keep them safe. Sometimes she is successful: when the fire has done its worst and died down, you may find a dead hen with live chicks underneath its wings.

Now imagine Jesus as the hen, and his fellow-Jews, not least the inhabitants of Jerusalem, as the chickens. What is Jesus saying he wanted to do?

To answer that, you have to understand the dark and threatening paragraph that comes before the final one (23.24–36). Jesus sees a build-up of guilt: the guilt of Israel, rejecting prophet after prophet, and stoning the people God has sent to warn them of danger. This is, of course, similar to what happens in the **parables** of the wicked tenant farmers and the wedding banquet (21.33–46; 22.1–14). Behind this, though, there is also the guilt of the whole human race. Jesus traces the line of blood-guilt back to the killing of Abel, the first victim of murder, killed by his brother Cain in Genesis 4. What can he mean? How can all this come upon one generation? And what does he propose to do about it?

The answer takes us, not into more denunciations, but deep into the heart of Jesus' own vocation and Matthew's biblical understanding of how it works. The key to it all is the way in which, within biblical theology, Israel was called to represent the rest of the world before God. Israel, said God to Moses at Sinai, was to be a nation of **priests** (Exodus 19.5–6), God's special people out of all the nations. But this was not for its own sake. Israel was to be God's special people in order to be the light of the nations (Isaiah 42.6; 49.6).

But if the world remained rebellious and wicked – as it showed every sign of doing – what would this vocation then mean? Isaiah, once more, came to the stunning prophetic vision that Israel, in the person of the Servant of the Lord, would bear in his own person the guilt and sin of everyone else. The darkness of the whole world would descend upon Israel itself, so that it might be dealt with and the world might after all have light (52.13—53.12).

Jesus himself, and the **gospel** writers as they reflected on his achievement, saw this picture coming to fulfilment in himself. His vocation was to draw on to himself the destiny of Israel, which in turn was to be the focal point of the whole world. (The fact that many, including many Christians, never learn to think like this is a measure of how far we have moved away from a truly biblical world-view.) The world had provoked its creator, worshipping idols and behaving in destructive, and self-destructive, patterns. Israel, called to bring God's light to the world, had instead copied the world. The whole human race had played with fire; and the fire was now raging out of control. Jesus, as the mother hen, longed to gather the chickens under his wings, to take the full force of the fire on to himself and rescue the chickens from it.

But they refused. And the fire, now blazing merrily, would rage on until the generation that had seen the Emmanuel, and had rejected his offer of rescue, had been consumed by its flames. This is not a way of saying, as the early church quickly came to say, that Jesus' own death did in fact save people from the ultimate consequences of their own choices. That would come later. This is a statement of what Jesus had longed to do, and of the consequences of Israel's refusing to allow him to do it.

In particular, the weight of judgment would fall on the **Temple**. 'Your house has been abandoned': in many passages in the Old Testament, the living God who had promised to live in the Temple in Jerusalem warns that persistent sin among his people will result in the withdrawal of his presence, leaving the Temple desolate, defenceless against enemy attack. That is what Jesus is now predicting, and the next chapter in the book will show what this will mean.

The final, sorrowful saying makes it clear that the messianic blessings that Jesus longed to bring to Israel can only be received by those who welcome him in **faith**. 'Blessed is the one who comes' is, to this day, the regular Hebrew way of saying 'welcome'. The point is then that the only way to profit from what Jesus is about to do is to speak with true understanding the words which the Palm Sunday crowds sang, albeit with a shallow view of **Messiahship** (21.9).

The saying haunts all subsequent telling of Jesus' story. Are we, the readers or hearers, really welcoming the true Jesus, the one who denounces evil and then takes it upon himself in the final great act of love? Or do we prefer, like the crowds a few days before, to welcome the 'Jesus' who happens to fit the imaginings and agendas that we have worked out for ourselves?

MATTHEW 24.1–14

The Beginning of the Birth Pangs

[1]Jesus left the Temple and went away. As he did so, his disciples came and pointed out the Temple buildings to him. [2]'Yes,' he said, 'and you see all these things? I'm telling you the truth: not one stone will be left standing upon another. All of them will be thrown down.'

[3]As he was sitting on the Mount of Olives, his disciples came to him privately.

'Tell us,' they said, 'when will these things happen? And what will be the sign that you are going to appear as king, and that the end of the age is upon us?'

[4]'Watch out,' replied Jesus. 'Don't let anyone deceive you. [5]You see, there will be several who will come along, using my name, telling you "I'm the Messiah!" They will fool lots of people. [6]You're going to hear about wars, actual wars and rumoured ones; make sure you don't get alarmed. This has got to happen, but it doesn't mean the end is coming yet. [7]Nations

will rise against one another, and kingdoms against each other. There will be famines and earthquakes here and there. [8]All this is just the start of the birthpangs.

[9]'Then they will hand you over to be tortured, and they will kill you. You will be hated by all nations because of my name. [10]Then several will find the going too hard, and they will betray each other and hate each other. [11]Many false prophets will arise, and they will deceive plenty of people. [12]And because lawlessness will be on the increase, many will find their love growing cold. [13]But the one who lasts out to the end will be delivered. [14]And this gospel of the kingdom must be announced to the whole world, as a witness to all the nations. Then the end will come.'

We went together to see the doctor, one rainy day in the autumn. We were excited but also very apprehensive. We had a sense of going down a road we'd often heard about but had never quite believed we would travel ourselves.

He talked us gently through the whole process. Yes, the first few months were sometimes difficult. People often felt sick, especially in the morning. There were some dangers during that time but it was normally under control. Then there would come a period of quite dramatic changes, as the new little life inside the womb made its presence felt. One would need to take care, especially with diet and with strenuous activities. Then at last, as the day grew nearer, there would be all sorts of things to watch out for: high blood pressure, various potential risks for the baby. And the birth itself: well, that was something else again, and we'd talk more about it nearer the time. But our task in the meantime was to take care, be patient, and not be alarmed by some of the strange things that were going to happen.

One of the greatest biblical images for God's future is the approaching birth of a baby. It is a time of great hope and new possibility, and also, especially before modern medicine, a time of great danger and anxiety. The medical profession can describe and study each stage of pregnancy in detail. But every couple, and of course particularly every mother, has to face them personally and live through them, even though for some it is a traumatic, painful and upsetting time. The biblical writers draw freely on this well-known experience to speak of the new world that God intends to bring to birth. And one of the high-water marks of this whole biblical theme is this chapter in Matthew, and its parallels in Mark (chapter 13) and Luke (chapter 21). This, said Jesus, is just the start of the birth pangs.

It's only with images like this that one can speak of God's future. We don't have an exact description of it, and we wouldn't be able to cope with it if we did. What we have are pictures: the birth of a baby, the marriage of a king's son, a tree sprouting new leaves. God's future will be like all these, and (of course) unlike them as well.

As far as Jesus is concerned, there are two central features of God's future. On the one hand, there is his own calling and destiny; he has spoken about it often enough in the last few chapters. He has come to Jerusalem knowing that by continuing his dramatic mission of summoning Israel to **repentance** he will precipitate hostility, violence and his own death. And he believes that God will vindicate him after his death, by raising him from the dead.

On the other hand, there was the fate of the Jerusalem **Temple**. Throughout his public career Jesus had done and said things which implied that he, not the Temple, was the real centre of God's healing and restoring work. Now he had done and said things in the Temple itself which implied that the whole place was under judgment and that he had the right to pronounce that judgment. And when the **disciples** pointed out to him the magnificent buildings (the Temple was generally recognized as one of the most beautiful sights in the whole world) he warned them explicitly: it was all going to come crashing down.

The disciples put two and two together. The destruction of the Temple on the one hand; on the other hand, the vindication of all that Jesus has said and done. Somehow they go with each other. If Jesus has been right all along, then the Temple will have to go. But how? And when? When will the world see that Jesus really is God's **Messiah**?

If you were a Roman citizen, believing that Caesar was the rightful king of the world, but living at some distance from Rome itself, you would long for the day when he would pay you a state visit. Not only would you see him for yourself, but, equally importantly, all your neighbours would realize that he really was the world's lord and master.

Much of the Roman empire was Greek-speaking; and the Greek word that they would use for such a state visit, such an 'appearing' or 'presence', was **parousia**. The same word was often used to describe what happens when a god or goddess did something dramatic – a healing **miracle**, say – which was thought to reveal their power and presence. And it's this word *parousia* which the disciples use in verse 3, when they ask Jesus about what's going to happen.

They speak of three things. Each is important in the long chapter that is now beginning, containing Jesus' answer to them: the destruction of the Temple, Jesus' *parousia* or 'appearance as king', and 'the end of the age'. Throughout this chapter we have to face the questions: What did they mean, what did Jesus mean in answering them, what did Matthew understand by it all – and what's it got to say to us? This calls for a cool head and an attentive mind.

For the moment we can begin to glimpse what Jesus thought it was all about. The disciples wanted to see him ruling as king, with all that that would mean, including the Temple's destruction and, indeed, the ushering in of God's new age. The **present age** would come to its convulsive conclusion, and the new age would be born. Well, Jesus says, there will indeed be convulsions. The birth pangs of the new age will start, in the form of wars, revolutions, famines and earthquakes. Terrible times are going to come, and those who follow him will be tested severely. Many will give it all up as just too demanding.

But they shouldn't be deceived. New would-be messiahs will appear, but the vindication of Jesus himself – his royal 'presence' or 'appearing' – won't be that sort of thing, someone else coming and leading a revolt. They must hold on, keep their nerve, and remain faithful. Between the present moment and the time when all will be revealed, and Jerusalem will be destroyed, the **good news** of the **kingdom of God** which Jesus came to bring will have to spread not just around Israel, as has been the case up to now (10.5–6; 15.24), but to the whole world. There is a task for them to do in the interim period.

All of this related very specifically to the time between Jesus' public career and the destruction of the Temple in AD 70. We shall see how it works out in the following passages. But the echoes of meaning rumble on in every successive generation of Christian discipleship. We too are called to be faithful, to hold on and not be alarmed. We too may be called to live through troubled times and to last out to the end. We too may see the destruction of cherished and beautiful symbols. Our calling then is to hold on to Jesus himself, to continue to trust him, to believe that the one who was vindicated by God in the first century will one day be vindicated before the whole world. We too are called to live with the birth pangs of God's new age, and to trust that in his good time the new world will be born.

MATTHEW 24.15–28

The Desolating Sacrilege

¹⁵'So when you see "the sacrilege that desolates", as Daniel the prophet put it, standing in the holy place (the reader should

understand), [16]then those who are in Judaea should take to their heels and run to the mountains. [17]If you're up on your roof, don't go down into the house to get things out. [18]If you're in the fields, don't go back to pick up your cloak. [19]It's going to be terrible for pregnant and nursing women during those days. [20]Pray that it won't be winter when you have to run away, or for that matter a sabbath. [21]Yes: there's going to be such great suffering then as has never been since the start of the world until now – no, and won't ever be again. [22]And if those days had not been shortened, nobody at all would have been rescued. But for the sake of God's chosen ones those days will be shortened.

[23]'Then if anyone says to you, "Look! Here is the Messiah!" or "Look! There he is!", don't believe them. [24]False messiahs will arise, you see, and false prophets too. They will provide great signs and portents, so as to deceive even God's chosen ones, if that were possible. [25]Remember, I'm telling you this beforehand!

[26]'So if someone says to you, "Look! He's out in the wilderness", don't go out. If they say, "Look, he's in the inner room", don't believe them. [27]You see, the royal appearing of the son of man will be like the lightning that comes from the east and flashes across to the west. [28]Where the carcass is, there the vultures will gather.'

In many countries, one of the things children look forward to is going away to a summer camp. The weather is warm, there is swimming and boating, there are old friends and new ones, there are songs round a campfire, there are sports and games and shows. Everyone – at least in theory – has a great time.

One of the games that some camps play is 'hunt the leader'. Two or three adults from the organizing team dress up in disguise, making themselves completely unrecognizable, and go into the local town. The children are then brought into the town, and have to go around and see if they can find the hidden leaders. This, of course, means looking at lots of people who aren't in disguise at all, but are just their normal selves. There are lots of wrong guesses. Eventually they find them, and suddenly it seems obvious: of course that's her! Yes, of course that's him! But at the time it seemed as though the disguise would deceive them for ever.

Jesus is warning the **disciples** that people will tell them again and again that the **Messiah** has come, and that if they look they will find him. They will be tempted to look at this leader or that leader – someone gathering followers out in the desert, someone else plotting in a secret room off a back alley – and wonder if it's really Jesus himself, returned in some form. It won't be, he says. When the true Messiah – himself, of course, – is revealed, then there will be no question. His 'royal appearing' (**parousia** again, in verse 27, as in the previous passage) will leave no room for doubt. You won't have to pierce any disguise. You will know.

The setting for all this is the sequence of events that will lead to the destruction of Jerusalem. Matthew, like Mark at this point, knows that the only way he can write of this is in the code of biblical imagery, and that the most appropriate source is the book of Daniel.

Daniel was an extremely popular book in the first century. Jesus drew on it freely, as did many of his contemporaries. It describes, in a series of stories and dreams, how God's **kingdom** will triumph over the kingdoms of the world. Daniel 2 is about the stone which smashes the great statue; we looked at that when reading 21.33–46. Chapters 3 and 6 are about how God delivers his faithful ones from suffering. Chapter 7, at the centre of the book, is about the monsters that wage war on the humans, and about how God vindicates the human figure ('one like a **son of man**') and destroys the monsters – which any first-century Jew would recognize as code for Israel being vindicated over the pagan nations.

Those are perhaps the best-known parts. But there is more.

Daniel 12 predicts the eventual **resurrection** of all God's people. And chapter 9 speaks of something blasphemous, sacrilegious, some abominable object, which will be placed in the **Temple** itself. This, it seems, will be part of the sequence of events through which God will redeem his true people, send his true Messiah, and bring his age-old plan to completion.

That's quite a lot to hold in your mind, but Matthew wants you to, because only so can you begin to wrestle with what Jesus was telling the disciples. Remember, the questions that dominate the chapter are: when is the **Temple** to be destroyed? When will Jesus be seen to be the Messiah? When will the **present age** be brought to its close? The answer here is: look back to Daniel, which speaks of all these things, and look out for the terrible time that's coming.

In particular, look out for the pagan invasion that will end up placing blasphemous objects in the Temple itself. This nearly happened within ten years of Jesus' own time. In AD 40, the Roman emperor Gaius Caligula tried to place a huge statue of himself in the Temple. He deliberately wanted to do this to snub and offend the Jews. In the end he was assassinated before it happened; but, had he gone ahead, all the events described in Matthew 24 could have happened right away. In fact, it was another 30 years before Roman legions surrounded the Temple and eventually placed their blasphemous standards there. That was indeed the beginning of the end for Jerusalem, the end of the world order that Jesus and his followers, and their ancestors for many generations, had known.

What should Jesus' followers do when all this happens? They should get out and run. Think about it: their natural tendency, as loyal Jews, might well have been to stay and fight, to join a new resistance movement and, yes, to sign up to fight for a new Messiah. They had, after all, come to Jerusalem with Jesus in the hope that there might be some kind of battle for the kingdom. In a couple of chapters we will see one of them waving a sword around in the darkness, assuming that Jesus wanted them to start fighting at last. But this isn't at all what Jesus has in mind. This is not how the kingdom of God will come. This is not how he will be vindicated both as a true prophet and as Messiah.

They must run away because Jerusalem itself is under God's judgment, and the pagan images in the Temple are the sign that the judgment is about to fall. Whatever other levels of 'salvation' there are in the New Testament, they must also include the very basic and physical: Jesus wants his people to be rescued from the destruction that is coming upon the city. When they see the signs, they are not to hang around, to collect up their property. They are to hurry at once, away from the city that has God's judgment hanging over it by a single thread. It will be a time of great suffering and hardship.

And when it all happens, there won't be any doubt. The event will not be disguised. You won't have to guess to see the Messiah being vindicated. He won't be standing there in person, maybe looking like somebody else. His vindication will be read in the signs of the times. Where the carcass is, there the vultures will gather: the ancient world didn't always distinguish between vultures and eagles, and when the eagles on the Roman standards gathered around Jerusalem they would seem like birds of prey circling over a corpse in the desert, coming in for the final kill.

Once again, the terrible times of the first century are echoed by the terrible times that the world, and the church, have had to go through many times over. As I write this I am conscious that some of my brother and sister Christians will today be running away from evil regimes, will be tortured and killed for their **faith**. They will be tempted to follow false messiahs who offer them quick solutions. But the passage is not primarily about us today. Its main significance lies in the fact that then, in the time of Jesus and the disciples, the world

119

went through its greatest convulsion of all, through which God's new world began to be born. Living with this fact, and working out its long-term implications, have been essential parts of Christian discipleship ever afterwards.

MATTHEW 24.29–35

The Coming of the Son of Man

[29]'Straight away,' Jesus continued, 'after the suffering that those days will bring,

> The sun will turn to darkness,
> And the moon won't give its light;
> The stars will fall from heaven,
> And the powers of heaven will shake.

[30]'And then the sign of the son of man will appear in heaven; then all the tribes of the earth will mourn. They will see "the son of man coming on the clouds of heaven" with power and great glory. [31]He will send off his messengers with a great trumpet-blast, and they will collect his chosen ones from the four winds, from one end of heaven to the other.

[32]'Learn the hidden meaning from the fig-tree. When its branch begins to sprout, and to push out its leaves, then you know that summer is nearly there. [33]So with you: when you see all these things, you will know that it is near, at the very gates. [34]I'm telling you the truth: this generation won't be gone before all these things happen. [35]Heaven and earth will disappear, but my words will never, ever disappear.'

A friend of mine is a composer. (It's something I would like to have been myself, had things worked out differently, so I take a particular interest in what he does.) I watched one day as he worked on a particular piece he was writing. The large sheet of music paper sat there in front of him, with a dozen or more sets of lines waiting for notes to be written on them.

He was, at that moment, writing the clarinet part. He had already pencilled in the violins, several staves below. There were a couple of scribbles where the brass would go, somewhere in between. He had an idea about the flute and piccolo, and a few notes in their part were already there to give an indication of what would be balancing the clarinet in the woodwind section.

I left him to it and got on with other things. An hour or two later we met for coffee, and he showed me the page. It was more or less complete. In order to make about fifteen seconds' worth of music, he had had to spend several hours writing out, one by one in turn, the individual line for each instrument. They would be heard all together, but they needed (of course) to be written out separately.

Now imagine that process in reverse. Listen to a short piece of music. It's over in a few seconds. But now go to the orchestra and ask the instruments to play their lines one after the other. There may well be several minutes between when the piccolo begins and when the double bass concludes. What is essentially one short piece of music could be spun out over quite some time.

Reading the sort of section now in front of us demands that sort of imagination. Often in the Bible there are passages in which several things have come rushing together into one short, tight-packed chord or musical sequence. But in order to understand them, we have to take them apart and allow them to be heard one after the other. Particularly when it comes to prophecy, the biblical writers often spoke of something which sounded as though it was all one event but which they knew might well be, and we know actually was, a sequence of events, one after the other.

The tune that this passage is playing is called 'the coming of the **son of man**'. In some parts of today's church, it's almost the only tune they sing, and I am concerned that they usually sing it in the wrong key. The orchestration is rich and dense. It needs looking at bit by bit.

Here's a bit from the prophet Isaiah. 'The sun will be darkened, the moon won't shine, the stars will fall from the sky, and the heavenly powers will be shaken.' What does that mean?

For Isaiah, and for those who read him in the first century, the one thing it didn't mean was something to do with the actual sun, moon and stars in the sky. That would make a quite different tune. This language was well known, regular code for talking about what we would call huge social and political convulsions. When we say that empires 'fall', or that kingdoms 'rise', we don't normally envisage any actual downward or upward physical movement. Matthew intends us to understand that the time of the coming of the son of man will be a time when the whole world seems to be in turmoil.

But what will this 'coming' itself actually *be*? What will Jesus' 'royal appearing' consist of? Matthew takes us back, in line with so much in Jesus' teaching, to the prophet Daniel again, and this time to the crucial passage in 7.13 (verse 30 in our present passage). They will see, he says, 'the son of man coming on the clouds of **heaven**'. Now in Daniel this certainly refers, not to a *downward* movement of this strange human figure, but to an *upward* movement. The son of man 'comes' from the point of view of the heavenly world, that is, he comes *from* earth *to* heaven. His 'coming' in this sense, in other words, is not his 'return' to earth after a sojourn in heaven. It is his ascension, his vindication, the thing which demonstrates that his suffering has not been in vain.

What is it, then, that will demonstrate that Jesus has been vindicated by God? Three things.

First, his **resurrection** and ascension. These great, dramatic, earth-shattering events will reverse the verdicts of the Jewish court and the pagan executioners. They will show that he is indeed 'the son of man' who has suffered at the hands of the 'beasts' or 'monsters' – who now, it seems, include the **Temple** and those who run it! – and is nevertheless then declared by God to be his true spokesman.

Second, the destruction of the Temple. Jesus, speaking as a prophet, predicted that it would fall, not as an arbitrary exercise of his prophetic powers but because the Temple had come to symbolize all that was wrong with the Israel of his day. And he had predicted the terrible suffering that would precede it. That's why, in verse 25, he underlines the fact that he has told them about it beforehand. They are to trust that he is a true prophet. They must not be deceived by the odd things that others may do to lead them astray. And when the Temple finally falls, that will be the sign that he was speaking the truth. That will be his real vindication. His exaltation over the world, and over the Temple, will be written in large letters into the pages of history; or, as they would put it, 'they will see the sign of the son of man in heaven' (verse 30).

Third, the news of his victory will spread rapidly throughout the world. What people will see is strange messengers, alone or in small groups, travelling around from country to country telling people that a recently executed Jewish prophet has been vindicated by God, that he is the **Messiah** and the Lord of the world. But that's just the surface event. The deeper dimension of these happenings is that the one true God is announcing to his whole creation that Jesus is his appointed Lord of the world. Or, as they would put it, 'he will send off his messengers' (or 'angels'), 'and collect his chosen ones from the four winds, from one end of heaven to the other'. If we are to understand the biblical writers, we have to learn, once again, to read their language in their way.

All this is spoken to Jesus' **disciples** so they will know when the cataclysmic events are going to happen. Watch for the leaves on the tree, and you can tell it's nearly summer. Watch for these events, and you'll know that the great event, the destruction of the Temple and Jesus' complete vindication, are just around the corner. And be sure of this, says Jesus (and Matthew wants to underline this): it will happen within a generation.

That is an extra important reason why everything that has been said in the passage so far must be taken to refer to the destruction of Jerusalem and the events that surround it. Only when we appreciate how significant that moment was for everything Jesus had said and done will we understand what Jesus himself stood for.

But remember the composer and the music. In the long purposes of God, we who read passages like this many centuries later may find that what was said as a single statement, one short piece of music, can then be played as a string of separate parts, one after the other. I see no reason why, once we are quite clear about its original meaning, we should not then see the chapter as a pointer to other events, to the time we still await when God will complete what he began in the first century, and bring the whole created order, as Paul promised in Romans 8, to share the liberty of the glory of God's children. As we look back to the first century, we should also look on to God's still-promised future, and thank him that Jesus is already enthroned as Lord of all time and history.

MATTHEW 24.36–44

The Unexpected Coming

³⁶'Nobody knows what day or time this will happen,' Jesus went on. 'The angels in heaven don't know it, and nor does the son; only the father knows. ³⁷You see, the royal appearing of the son of man will be like the days of Noah.

³⁸'What does that mean? Well, in those days, before the flood, they were eating and drinking, they were getting married and giving children in marriage, right up to the day when Noah went into the ark. ³⁹They didn't know about it until the flood

124

came and swept them all away. That's what it'll be like at the royal appearing of the son of man.

40'On that day there will be two people working in the field. One will be taken, the other will be left. 41There will be two women grinding corn in the mill. One will be taken, the other will be left.

42'So keep alert! You don't know what day your Master will come. 43But bear this in mind: if the householder had known what time of night the burglar was going to come, he would have stayed awake and wouldn't have let his house get broken into. 44So you too must be ready! The son of man is coming at a time you don't expect.'

It was a fine Saturday afternoon in the heat of summer. The family, some on holiday from work, were relaxing in the house and the garden. Books and magazines were lying around the place, along with coffee mugs, newspapers and packets of biscuits. Everything had the look of the sort of cheerful untidiness that a large family can create in about an hour.

Suddenly there was a ring at the doorbell. Wondering vaguely which friend might be calling I went to answer it, dressed as I was in very casual clothes. There, outside, to my horror, was a party of 30 or so well-dressed visitors. They had arranged, many months before, to come to look at the house, because of its historic associations. And neither I nor the family had remembered a thing about it.

You can imagine the next five minutes. I suggested that the visitors went into the garden for a little while ('to get a good look at the house from the outside'), and then mobilized the family to clear everything up. Within minutes everything was clean and tidy. The children retreated into bedrooms. We opened the front door again and the visit went ahead.

You can tidy a house in a few minutes, if you put your mind to it. But you can't reverse the direction of a whole life, a whole culture. By the time the ring on the doorbell happens it's too late. That's what this passage, and the next one, are about.

Once again it has been applied to two different kinds of event, neither of which was what Jesus himself had in mind (though some think Matthew was already looking further ahead). We had better look at them first.

On the one hand, a great many readers have seen here a warning to Christians to be ready for the second coming of Jesus. This goes, obviously, with an interpretation of the earlier part of the chapter which sees the 'coming' of the **son of man** not as his vindication, his exaltation to **heaven**, but as his return to earth. We have been promised, in Acts 1, 1 Thessalonians 4, and many, many other passages, that one day, when God remakes the entire world, Jesus himself will take centre stage. He will 'appear' again, as Paul and John put it (e.g. Colossians 3.4; 1 John 3.2). Since nobody knows when that will be, it is vital that all Christians should be ready all the time.

On the other hand, many other readers have seen here a warning to Christians to be ready for their own death. Whatever precisely one thinks will happen immediately after death – and that's a subject devout Christians have often disagreed about – it's clearly important that we should, in principle, be ready for that great step into the unknown, whenever it is asked of us. That's one of many reasons why keeping short accounts with God, through regular worship, prayer, reading of scripture, self-examination and Christian obedience, matters as much as it does.

You can read the passage in either of these ways, or both. Often the voice of God can be heard in scripture even in ways the original writers hadn't imagined – though you need to retain, as the control, a clear sense of what they *did* mean, in case you make scripture 'prove' all kinds of things which it certainly doesn't. It is vital, therefore, to read the passage as it would have been heard by Matthew's first audience. And there, it seems, we are back to the great crisis that was going to sweep over Jerusalem and its surrounding countryside at a date that was, to them, in the unknown future – though we now know it happened in AD 70, at the climax of the war between Rome and Judaea. Something was going to happen which would devastate lives, families, whole communities: something that was both a terrible, frightening event and also, at the same time, the event that was to be seen as 'the coming of the son of man' or the **parousia**, the 'royal appearing' of Jesus himself. And the whole passage indicates what this will be. It will be the swift and sudden sequence of events that will end with the destruction of Jerusalem and the **Temple**.

The point this passage makes comes in three stages:

First, nobody knows exactly when this will be; only that it will be within a generation (verse 34).

Second, life will go on as normal right up to the last minute. That's the point of the parallel with the time of Noah. Until the flood came to sweep everything away (is Matthew remembering 7.26–27?), ordinary life was carrying on with nothing unusual.

Third, it will divide families and work colleagues down the middle. 'One will be taken and one left'; this doesn't mean (as some have suggested) that one person will be 'taken' away by God in some kind of supernatural salvation, while the other is 'left' to face destruction. If anything, it's the opposite: when invading forces sweep through a town or village, they will 'take' some off to their deaths, and 'leave' others untouched.

The result – and this is the point Jesus is most anxious to get across to his **disciples**, who by this stage must have been quite puzzled as to where it was all going – is that his followers must stay awake, like people who know there are going to be surprise visitors coming sooner or later but who don't know exactly when. What this means in detail, the next passage will explain.

The warning was primarily directed to the situation of dire

emergency in the first century, after Jesus' death and **resurrection** and before his words about the Temple came true. But they ring through subsequent centuries, and into our own day. We too live in turbulent and dangerous times. Who knows what will happen next week, next year? It's up to each church, and each individual Christian, to answer the question: are you ready? Are you awake?

MATTHEW 24.45–51

The Wise and Wicked Slaves

[45]'So,' Jesus went on, 'who's going to play the part of the trustworthy and sensible slave, the one the master will set over his household, so that he will give them their meals at the right time? [46]It's good news for the servant whom the master finds doing just that when he comes. [47]I'm telling you the truth: he'll promote him to be over all his belongings. [48]But if the wicked slave says in his heart, "My master's taking his time", [49]and starts to beat the other slaves, and to feast and drink with the drunkards, [50]the master of that slave will come on a day he doesn't expect, and at a time he doesn't know. [51]He will cut him in two, and put him along with the hypocrites, where people will weep and grind their teeth.'

The managing director was returning from a meeting out of town, when he saw a familiar but unexpected sight. There, turning out of a street ahead of him, was one of his own company's vans. What was it doing here? The company didn't do business with anyone in this part of the town. What was going on?

He took the number of the van, and later in the day called the driver in. He confessed. He'd been moonlighting – working for another company at the same time, while he was supposed to be making deliveries for the company which owned the vans. He'd been, in that sense, a hypocrite, a play-actor, pretending to be one thing while in fact being another. That was his last day working for that company.

Of course, today they put electronic components into trucks and vans which record everything that happens – speed, rest periods, fuel consumption, you name it. 'The spy in the cab', the drivers call it, resentfully. But at least they know they aren't going to get away with cheating. No chance of the boss suddenly coming upon them doing something they shouldn't.

The scene changes once again, as it has done throughout Matthew 24, and will again in Matthew 25. But the underlying drama is the same. This time we imagine a householder going away on business and coming back suddenly: will he find the workers (in that world, the slaves) doing what they should, or not? As we've seen several times, in that world a story about a master and servants would almost certainly be understood as a story about God and Israel. God has left Israel with tasks to perform; when he comes back, what will his verdict be on how they have accomplished them?

At the same time, there may be here a further twist to this plot, from the point of view of Jesus speaking to the **disciples** on the Mount of Olives. He is going to leave them with work to do: the **gospel** must be announced to all the nations (24.14). Some of them will have responsibilities within the young and struggling Christian community. How will they discharge them?

The options presented here are stark. The slave in charge of the household has duties, and must do them. If he thinks to himself that his master won't be back for a long while yet, and decides to live it up, have a good time, and (for good measure) ill-treat his fellow-slaves, he will be in deep trouble. He will be a play-actor, a hypocrite. He will be pretending to be one thing while being another. And, once again the familiar and terrifying refrain: such people will find themselves outside, in the dark, where people weep and grind their teeth (8.12; 13.42, 50; 22.13; and, still to come, 25.30).

The difference between the two types of slave – the one who kept watch and did what he should, and the one who forgot what he was about and did the opposite – isn't just the difference between good and bad, between obedience and disobedience. It's the difference between wisdom and folly. This either/or is going to dominate the next story as well, and it's worth taking a minute to notice where it comes from.

Deep within ancient Jewish tradition we find the book of Proverbs. There, mostly in short sayings but sometimes in more extended pictures, we find in a wealth of detail the contrast between the wise person and the foolish person. Of course, ultimately the wise person is the one who respects and honours God, and the fool is the one who forgets him. But their wisdom and folly work themselves out in a thousand different ways in daily life, in business, in the home and village, in making plans for the future, in how they treat other people, in their honesty or dishonesty, in their hard work or laziness, in their ability to recognize and avoid temptations to immorality. Jesus is here invoking this whole tradition of wisdom-writing, which continued to develop in Judaism after the Old Testament, and which came into early Christianity in books like the letter of James. We've seen it already in Matthew, at a significant moment: the wise builder built the house on rock, the foolish one built it on sand (7.24–27).

But now the point of 'wisdom' and 'folly' is not just being able to do what God wants in any and every situation. If the living God might knock at the door at any time, wisdom means being ready at any time. What's more, once Jesus has come, bringing God's **kingdom** to bear on the world, being wise or being foolish means knowing, or not knowing, what time it is in God's timetable. Wisdom consists not least, now, in realizing that the world has turned a corner with the coming of Jesus and that we must always be ready to give an account of ourselves.

Of course these warnings are held within the larger picture of the gospel, in which Jesus embodies the love of God which goes out freely to all and sundry. Of course we shall fail. Of course there will be times when we shall go to sleep on the job. Part of being a follower of Jesus is not that we always get everything right, but that, like Peter among others, we quickly discover where we are going wrong, and take steps to put it right.

But along with the welcome for sinners which Jesus announces, and the ready forgiveness that is always on offer when we fail and then come to our senses, there is the hard and high call to watchfulness and loyalty. You can't use God's grace as an excuse for going slack ('God will forgive me,' said one philosopher, 'that's his job'). Even when we don't think we're being watched, we can never forget that much is expected of those to whom much is given.

MATTHEW 25.1–13

The Wise and Foolish Girls

¹'Then,' continued Jesus, 'the kingdom of heaven will be like ten girls who each took their own torches and went out to meet the bridegroom. ²Five of them were silly, and five were sensible. ³The silly ones took their torches, but didn't take oil with them. ⁴The sensible ones took oil, in flasks, along with their torches.

⁵'The bridegroom took his time coming, and they all nodded off and went to sleep. ⁶In the middle of the night a shout went up: "Here's the bridegroom! Come on and meet him!" ⁷Then all the girls got up and trimmed the wicks of their torches.

⁸'The silly ones said to the sensible ones, "Give us some of your oil! Our torches are going out!"

⁹'But the sensible ones answered, "No! If we do that, there won't be enough for all of us together! You'd better go to the dealers and buy some for yourselves."

[10]'So off they went to buy oil. But, while they were gone, the bridegroom arrived. The ones who were ready went in with him to the wedding party, and the door was shut.

[11]'Later on the other girls came back. "Master, master!" they said, "open the door for us!"

[12]'"I'm telling you the truth," he said, "I don't know you."

[13]'So keep awake! You don't know the day or the hour.'

The guests had all arrived and were seated. The organ was playing. The bridegroom and the best man had been there half an hour in advance. The photographers were waiting. The flowers had all been beautifully arranged. The choir had practised their anthems. And the bride was nowhere to be seen.

Since I was supposed to be performing the service that day I went out of the church, and round the corner on to the street. Then I saw her. Her car was stuck in traffic a few hundred yards away. Eventually she and her bridesmaids had decided to walk. They were coming down the street. I stepped out into the road, in my full clerical robes, and held up the traffic. Cars hooted their horns. People waved and shouted 'good luck'. And we began the service a full 15 minutes late.

Every culture has its own way of celebrating a wedding – and its own risks of getting things wrong. I once knew a family where people were so afraid of a car breaking down on the way to the church that they hired a second one to drive behind the first, empty, just in case. But in different cultures the risks will be different. In the Middle East to this day there are all sorts of traditional customs for what is after all one of the most important transitional moments in human life, when two people leave the security of their respective families and publicly declare that they are going to begin to live as a new, different family.

In the Middle East, to this day, there are some places where the customs at a wedding are quite similar to the ones described here. In the modern West, people don't normally get married in the middle of the night! But in that culture torchlight processions, late in the evening, are certainly known, and it seems as though the proceedings might have several stages, with the bridegroom likely to be delayed at an earlier venue before he arrives for the banquet itself, to be greeted at last by the bridesmaids.

So much for the local colour of this story, which otherwise might be confusing for people used to other customs. What else is going on here? What does this **parable** add to the repeated warnings Jesus has already given about the need to be ready?

Even more obviously than the previous one, this story is rooted in the Jewish tradition of contrasting wisdom and folly – being sensible or being silly. The writer of Proverbs treats Wisdom and Folly as two women, and describes them calling out to men going by, and offering them their respective lifestyles. Now, in this story, Lady Wisdom and Mistress Folly have each become five young girls, and the story invites its hearers to decide which they'd rather be. Obviously, wisdom in this case means being ready with the oil for the lamp, and folly means not thinking about it until it's too late.

It's probably wrong to try to guess what the oil in the story 'stands for' (some have suggested that it means good works; others **faith**, or love, or almost any of the Christian virtues). It isn't that kind of story. Within the world of the story itself, it simply means being ready for the key moment. You can't squash all these parables together and make the details fit with each other; *all* the girls in this parable, including the 'wise' ones, go to sleep in verse 5, whereas in verse 13 Jesus tells his followers to stay awake. Again, that kind of detailed question misses the point. What matters is being ready; being prepared; being wise; thinking ahead, realizing that a crisis is coming sooner or later and that if you don't make preparations now, and keep them in good shape in the meantime, you'll wish you had.

There is one other aspect to this particular story which has roots deep in the Jewish context and has given rise to a tradition of hymn-writing about the coming of the bridegroom. Already in Matthew's **gospel** Jesus has referred to himself as the bridegroom (9.15). In a previous parable Jesus spoke of the **kingdom** as being like a king making a marriage feast for his son (22.2). Mention of a bridegroom hints again at Jesus' messiahship, which was of course a central issue in the previous chapters, ever since Jesus arrived in Jerusalem.

This highlights the fact that the parable isn't just about the very end of time, the great and terrible day for which the world and the church still wait. Throughout his ministry, Jesus was coming as **Messiah** to his people, Israel. They were the ones invited to the wedding feast. They, in this story, are divided between the wise, who know Jesus and make sure they keep alert for his 'coming', and the foolish, to whom at the end Jesus will say 'I don't know you' (verse 12, echoing 7.23). Just as the Sermon on the Mount summarizes, not Jesus' teaching to the subsequent church, but Jesus' challenge to the Israel of his own day, so these parables, towards the close of the final great discourse in Matthew's gospel, should probably be read in the same way, at least in their most basic meaning.

It is tempting to move away from this conclusion, because saying that parts of Jesus' teaching related particularly to a unique situation in his own time might make it look as though they are irrelevant for every other time. But that's not so. It is because what Jesus did was unique and decisive, changing for ever the way the world is and how God relates to it, that we have entered a new era in which his sovereign rule is to be brought to bear on the world. And in this new era, no less than in the unique time of Jesus and his first followers, we need as much as ever the warning that it's easy to go slack on the job, to stop paying attention to God's work and its demands, to be unprepared when the moment suddenly arrives.

MATTHEW 25.14–30

The Parable of the Talents

[14]'This is what it will be like,' Jesus went on. 'It will be like a man who was going off on a journey. He summoned his slaves, and handed over control of his property to them. [15]He gave five talents to the first, two to the next, and one to the last – each according to his ability. Then he left.

'Straight away [16]the man who had been given the five talents went out and traded with them, and made five more. [17]Similarly, the one who had received two talents went and made another two. [18]But the one who received a single talent went and dug a hole in the ground, and hid his master's money.

[19]'After a long time, the master of those slaves came back and settled accounts with them. [20]The man who had received five talents came forward and gave him the other five talents. "Master," he said, "you gave me five talents. Look: I've made another five!" [21]"Well done indeed," said his master. "You're an excellent slave, and loyal too! You've been trustworthy with small things, and now I'm going to put you in charge of bigger ones. Come and join your master's celebration!"

[22]'Then the man who had had the two talents came forward. "Master," he said, "you gave me two talents. Look: I've made another two!" [23]"Well done indeed," said his master. "You're an excellent slave, and loyal too! You've been trustworthy with small things, and now I'm going to put you in charge of bigger ones. Come and join your master's celebration!"

[24]'Then the man who had had the one talent came forward. "Master," he said, "I knew that you were a hard man. You reap where you didn't sow, and you profit from things you never invested in. [25]So I was scared! I went and hid your talent in the ground. Here it is: it's yours, you can have it back."

135

²⁶"'You're a wicked and lazy slave!' answered his master. "So! You knew that I reap where I didn't sow, and profit from investments I never made? ²⁷Then you should have put my money with the bankers, and when I got back I would have received back what I had with interest!

²⁸"'So take the talent from him,' he went on, "and give it to the man who has ten talents." ²⁹(If someone already has something, you see, they will be given more, and they'll have plenty. But if someone has nothing, even what they have will be taken away from them.) ³⁰"But as for this useless slave, throw him outside in the dark, where people weep and grind their teeth.'"

As I write this, all over this country there are students – including one of my own children – who are taking examinations. In some cases these are not particularly serious. They will merely give the teachers and pupils a sense of how much work has been done, what has been learned and what has been forgotten, and where the work of the next school year needs to begin. But for others this is a life-changing moment. Everything they have done for the last year or two is being assessed, and the results will determine the course of the rest of their lives: what sort of job they will get, where they will live, and a thousand other things large and small.

There is always a danger that people will regard Christianity, and for that matter Judaism, as a kind of heavenly examination system. God, so people think, has given us a syllabus to study, things to learn and do, rules to keep. One day he'll come and set the final examination, and see who passes and who fails. Maybe there will be specially good things in store for people who get specially good marks, and likewise specially bad things for people with bad marks. And at first sight a **parable** like this one simply reinforces that impression.

But of course the whole of Jesus' ministry should make us protest against such a view of Christianity, of the **gospel**, of God himself. Jesus declared that he had come to call, not the righteous, but sinners. He had come, he said, to seek and to save the lost. He warned the **scribes** and **Pharisees** that the tax-collectors and prostitutes – who would have failed any examination that the Judaism of their day would have set! – would be going into the **kingdom of heaven** ahead of them. And he spent what in Matthew is an entire chapter (23) telling the self-appointed leaders of the Jewish people how dangerous it was simply to think of things in terms of all the rules they had to try to keep.

So what is this parable about?

The normal way of taking it is to suggest that Jesus is preparing the **disciples** for quite a long period during which he will not be present, and will have left them tasks to be getting on with. On his return they will be judged according to how they have performed. That, of course, can easily collapse into the 'examination-system' understanding of Christianity once more. It doesn't have to, but it easily could.

But the real problem with it is that a story about a master and slaves, in which the master goes away leaving the slaves tasks to perform and then comes back at last, would certainly be understood, in the Judaism of Jesus' day, as a story about God and Israel. This is certainly how Luke intends us to understand the very similar story in his gospel (19.11–27). And if, as I've suggested all along, both the Sermon on the Mount and this final great discourse in Matthew's gospel are to be seen first and foremost as Jesus' challenge to his own day and the days immediately following, perhaps we should take this parable in the same way.

It then belongs closely with Matthew 23, where Jesus denounces the scribes and Pharisees. They, we may suggest, are represented by the wicked servant who hid his master's money. (A 'talent', by the way, was a unit of money, worth roughly what a labourer could earn in 15 years. Our modern word 'talent', in the sense of the gifts or skills that an individual possesses, is derived from this, precisely because of this parable.) In what sense had they been given something that corresponds to the gift of the talent?

The scribes and Pharisees had been given the **law** of Moses. They had been given the **Temple**, the sign of God's presence among them. They had been given wonderful promises about how God would bless not only Israel but, through Israel, the whole world. And they had buried them in the ground. They had turned the command to be the light of the world into an encouragement to keep the light for themselves (5.14–16). They had been worthless slaves. And now, when their master was at last coming back, he was going to call them to account. The threatened destruction of Jerusalem and the Temple was to be seen as the master's punishment on the servant who had not done his will.

The emphasis of the parable falls, again and again, on this third slave, the one whose folly fails to respond to the master's generosity. Who then are the other two, those who respond appropriately to the master's trust?

They are, it seems, those who hear the call of Jesus and, on that basis, develop what Israel has already been given so that it now becomes something new. They are like the mustard seed in 13.31–32, which starts small and then grows large. They are the signs that God's kingdom is starting to bud and blossom. And now, when Jesus has come to Jerusalem to force the final confrontation between God's kingdom and the system that had resisted and opposed it – then those who are loyal to him will be like those who have made wise use of the money that had been entrusted to them.

This setting means that any sense of a 'final examination' is placed within a larger context, in which the grace and love of God are overflowing at every point. Yes, God does indeed long for people to use wisely the gifts they have been given. Yes, God did indeed come, in the person of the Emmanuel, Jesus the **Messiah,** to find out who within his chosen people had used profitably the blessings he had showered upon them. And, yes, once we have said this we can perfectly reasonably say, in line with the whole New Testament, that God will, still through the person of Jesus, sift and weigh everything that Christians do in the present life (see particularly 1 Corinthians 3.10–15; 2 Corinthians 5.10). All this is important and cannot be ignored.

But we must also, and always, insist that this parable and others like it do not give a complete picture of the creator God, the maker and lover of the world, the God who sent Jesus as the personal expression of his love. Remember where this parable occurs. It comes near the end of a story which is about to reach its great climax; and that climax comes when the **son of man** 'gives his life as a ransom for many' (20.28). When Jesus speaks of someone being thrown into the darkness outside, where people weep and grind their teeth, we must never forget that he was himself on the way into the darkness, where even he would sense himself abandoned by God (27.45–46).

MATTHEW 25.31–46

The Sheep and the Goats

[31]'When the son of man comes in his glory,' Jesus went on, 'and all the angels with him, then he will sit on his glorious throne. [32]All the nations will be assembled in front of him, and he will separate them from one another, like a shepherd separates the sheep from the goats. [33]He will stand the sheep at his right hand, and the goats at his left.

[34]'Then the king will say to those on his right, "Come here, you people who my father has blessed. Inherit the kingdom prepared for you from the foundation of the world! [35]Why? Because I was hungry and you gave me something to eat. I was thirsty and you gave me something to drink. I was a stranger and you made me welcome. [36]I was naked and you clothed me;

139

I was sick and you looked after me; I was in prison and you came to me."

37'Then the righteous will answer him, "Master, when did we see you hungry and feed you, or thirsty and give you a drink? 38When did we see you a stranger and welcome you, or naked and clothe you? 39When did we see you sick or in prison and come to see you?"

40'Then the king will answer them, "I'm telling you the truth: when you did it to one of the least significant of my brothers and sisters here, you did it to me."

41'Then he will say to those on his left hand, "Get away from me! You're accursed! Go to the everlasting fire prepared for the devil and his angels! 42Why? Because I was hungry and you gave me nothing to eat! I was thirsty and you gave me nothing to drink! 43I was a stranger and you didn't welcome me; I was naked and you didn't clothe me; I was sick and in prison and you didn't look after me!"

44'Then they too will answer, "Master, when did we see you hungry or thirsty, or a stranger, or naked, or sick, or in prison, and didn't do anything for you?"

45'Then he will answer them, "I'm telling you the truth: when you didn't do it for one of the least significant of my brothers and sisters here, you didn't do it to me."

46'And they will go away into everlasting punishment, but the righteous will go into everlasting life.'

One of the most remarkable things to happen in the whole twentieth century was the establishment of an International Court of Justice, located at The Hague in the Netherlands. Not everyone approves of such a thing, but whatever your opinion you must admit that it represents an astonishing leap forward in the way the world conducts its affairs.

Until recently even the concept of international law was a puzzle. But in the last century we have seen not only increasingly easy communication, but increasing awareness of massive and horrible crimes against humanity. The worldwide community has come together and declared that we will not stand there and watch injustice flourish.

Justice is one of the most profound longings of the human race. If there is no justice, then deep within ourselves we know that something is out of joint. Justice is hard to define and harder still to put into practice; but that has never stopped human beings and societies seeking it, praying for it, and working to find ways of doing it better. And 'justice' doesn't simply mean 'punishing wickedness', though that is regularly involved. It means bringing the world back into balance.

Central to the Jewish and Christian traditions (and some others; but these are the ones we're concerned with here) is the belief that this passionate longing for justice comes from the creator God himself. Jews and Christians believe that he will eventually do justice on a worldwide scale, in a way that the International Court can only dream of. God's judgment will be seen to be just. The world will be put to rights.

Part of the biblical image of the coming of the **son of man** is the announcement that justice will at last be done. There are many scenes in biblical and other Jewish literature which are like the present one. In this final part of Jesus' fifth and last discourse in Matthew's **gospel**, we have, not a **parable** as such, but another heavenly scene corresponding to, and indeed developing, the ones we had in chapter 24. Jesus is to be exalted as the ruler of the world, vindicated after his suffering. (The passage assumes the point we stressed earlier, that he has been exalted to a position of honour.) What we are now invited to witness is the way in which his just rule will be exercised.

The reference to sheep and goats, and to the shepherd who divides them up at the end of the grazing day (verses 32–33), is incidental to the main point, however much it has caught the imagination of readers. In the Middle East, to this day, sheep and goats regularly graze together, but need to be separated at night so that the goats, being less hardy, can be kept warm. It's often quite difficult to tell them apart. They can be similar in colour, but one main difference is that the sheep's tail hangs down and the goat's sticks up.

So what is the scene about?

At one level it is about the 'last judgment'. Western Christians at least are so familiar with this idea from paintings, mystery plays, and many classical writings that it's hard for us to get behind the tradition and see what is really being said. The criterion imposed for the judgment is an interesting one. Everything hinges on the way in which those who are judged have treated 'one of the least of these my brothers and sisters'. Who are these 'brothers and sisters', and who is being judged?

Jesus has earlier defined his brothers and sisters as 'those who do the will of my father in **heaven**', in a context which points to this as meaning 'those who hear and obey my **kingdom**-announcement' (12.50). The likely meaning of the scene, then, is that those who have not followed Jesus the **Messiah** will be judged in terms of how they have treated the people whom he counts as his family.

Of course, this doesn't mean that Christians themselves are not to behave in a similar way towards others. This may be taken for granted. But that is not what this scene is about. Just because we come to a passage with certain expectations, we shouldn't twist its details to fit.

The scene is the climax of a long discourse in which Jesus has denounced his own people, especially their would-be leaders, for their failure to live as God's people should, and has spoken of his own coming exaltation in accordance with the biblical picture of the vindication of the son of man. In that context, what we have here is a refocusing of one regular Jewish way of talking about God's judgment of the world.

Instead of the nations being judged on how they had treated Israel, as some Jewish writings envisage, Jesus, consistently with his whole redefinition of God's people around himself, declares that he will himself judge the world on how it has treated his *renewed* Israel. Judging the nations is, of course, regularly thought of as part of the Messiah's task (e.g. Psalm 2.8–12); and the king or Messiah is often pictured as a shepherd (e.g. Ezekiel 34.23–24). That, perhaps, is why the image of sheep and goats is inserted into this scene of judgment.

But when is Jesus seated on his throne, with all his angels in attendance? We have already glimpsed this scene, in 16.27. And I have suggested that the vindication of the son of man spoken of in 24.30 refers, not to his future second coming, but (as Jesus there insists) to the events which were to take place within a generation. According to the rest of the New Testament, not least St Paul, Jesus is *already* ruling the world as its rightful lord (e.g. 1 Corinthians 15.25–28). Should we not say, then, that this scene of judgment, though in this picture it is spoken of as a one-off, future and final event, may actually refer to what is happening throughout human history, from the time of Jesus' **resurrection** and ascension to the present? Could it be that the final judgment, in some sense, comes forward to meet us?

This is not to say, of course, that there will not also be a final moment when all judgment is complete, when, as the hymn says,

> Justice shall be throned in might,
> And every hurt be healed.

That, after all, is likewise insisted on by Paul and others (e.g. Romans 2.16; 2 Corinthians 5.10). But it is to say that, here at least, Jesus is portrayed as launching his followers on their dangerous and vulnerable mission as his brothers and sisters, with the knowledge that he, their older brother, is already ruling the world and taking note of what they suffer.

Does this seem, from the perspective of comfortable Western Christianity, smug or self-centred? Not if we think of the many places where the brothers and sisters of Jesus are treated, even today, with contempt, abuse, torture and death. That may help us to realize what an encouragement this passage must have been to Matthew's first readers, and what hope it could bring to many in our own day.

MATTHEW 26.1–13

Preparations for Jesus' Death

[1]So this is how it finally happened.

When Jesus had finished all these sayings, he said to his disciples, [2]'In two days' time, as you know, it'll be Passover! That's when the son of man will be handed over to be crucified.'

[3]Then the chief priests got together with the elders of the people, in the official residence of the high priest, who was called Caiaphas. [4]They plotted how to capture Jesus by some trick, and kill him.

[5]'We'd better not try anything at the feast,' they said. 'We don't want the people to riot.'

[6]While Jesus was at Bethany, in the house of Simon the leper, [7]a woman came to him who had an alabaster vase of extremely valuable ointment. She poured it on his head as he was reclining at the table.

[8]When the disciples saw it, they were furious.

'What's the point of all this waste?' they said. [9]'This could have been sold for a fortune, and the money could have been given to the poor!'

[10]Jesus knew what they were thinking.

'Why make life difficult for the woman?' he said. 'It's a lovely thing, what she's done for me. [11]You always have the poor with you, don't you? But you won't always have me. When she poured this ointment on my body, you see, she did it to prepare me for my burial. [13]I'm telling you the truth: wherever this gospel is announced in all the world, what she has just done will be told, and people will remember her.'

I stood at the bottom of the rock face. It was cold. The sun never penetrated that side of the mountain. I looked at the massive boulders around the foot of the climb, and then let my eye wander up the different routes, made famous by television programmes and glossy books as well as in specialist climbing literature. Up, and up, and up went the rock. I could just make out, as tiny coloured dots way above me, two or three groups of climbers. Some had started in the small hours that morning. One group had obviously begun the previous day. They had spent the night tied to the rock half a mile up, and were now making further progress.

I couldn't see the summit. There were clouds swirling around it. Though the forecast was good for later in the day, it was notorious that the weather could change suddenly, particularly up at the top.

Of all the mountains in Switzerland, the Eiger is the most stunning in its sheer, massive bulk. Its north face, at whose foot I was standing, looks as though some enormous giant had taken an axe and sliced through the mountain range, cutting away what might have been an ordinary, more gentle northern side, sloping down with meadows and woodland. Instead, what is left is this shocking vertical wall of bare rock, more than a mile high, blocking out the sun, simultaneously compelling and terrifying. I am drawn to it as by a magnet. Though my climbing days are long past, I can well understand why people want to spend days risking their lives to attempt it.

That is how we should feel as we stand at the foot of the final ascent of St Matthew's **gospel**. We have walked at a steady pace through the hills and valleys of the story. We have sat down to hear Jesus deliver another **parable** or discourse. We have marched with him along the road, enjoying the sunshine of the early days in Galilee, and the remarkable views as the **disciples** gradually realized more of what the **kingdom** was about. We have arrived in Jerusalem and watched dramatic events unfold. But we are now standing in front of a sheer wall of rock, and if we don't find it both compelling and terrifying we haven't got the right spectacles on.

The death of Jesus of Nazareth is one of the most famous and formative events in human history. There is a lot to be said, before you begin to study it line by line, for first running your eye right up the wall of rock, for reading the next two chapters through at a single sitting, with the door shut and the telephone turned off. Allow the whole thing to make its proper impact on you.

The way Matthew has told it, the story is dizzying. Instead of the gentle mountain slope that might have been there – Jesus, after confronting the authorities, going off back to Galilee to talk of the birds of the sky and the lilies of the field, to teach people to pray, to become a venerable old prophet with a long grey beard – it is as though a giant has sliced through the story with an axe from top to bottom, leaving, like dark exposed rock, the raw emotions, the longings and the horrors, of dozens of individuals and, out beyond them, of Israel, of the world, of ourselves.

The top isn't always visible. It's often hidden in the clouds. I have spent most of my life trying to pray, think, speak and write about the meaning of the death of Jesus; and, to be honest, some days I think I can see it clearly and other days I can't. Mountains are like that, and so is theology. That doesn't mean you can't be sure that it's there and that it really matters. If you thought the summit of the Eiger was only 'there' when it wasn't shrouded in mist, you'd be making a bad mistake. The theories about why Jesus died – theories of the 'atonement', as they are called – are like maps or old photographs, taken from a distance. They may be accurate in their way, and they're helpful particularly when it's cloudy and you can't see too much for the moment. But they're not the same thing as climbing to the top yourself, and perhaps, if you're lucky, getting there on a clear day when you can see the view. When that happens, you will find you quickly run out of words to describe what you are looking at.

As with any mountain, there are always people who tried to climb it, who got halfway up, thought better of it, and came back to declare that it was impossible and not worth doing anyway. Some people, including (alas) some within the church, would do anything rather than stand at the top of this mile-high rock, looking squarely at the death of Jesus in all its stark horror, and letting its beauty and terror captivate them for ever. But believe me, it's worth it. And Matthew is a great guide, if we will let him take us step by step.

The steps he shows us include a remarkable cast of characters, each of whom helps us a little way further towards the summit. Sometimes stories in the gospels are really only about Jesus and one or two others, but these two chapters are swarming with extra people. We hear their voices, see them plotting and squabbling and pontificating and weeping. We sense their excitement and panic, their politicking and puzzlement, their shock and trauma and hatred and hope.

Matthew allows each of them their say, and keeps them in balance: the central characters like Caiaphas and Peter, the walk-on parts like Pilate's wife and the servant-girls who point at Peter, the dark figure of Judas and the angry blaspheming pair crucified alongside Jesus. They are all drawn into the drama of the central character whose fate towers over the whole climb. As you read this story, there will almost certainly be someone you can identify with, someone you can come alongside as we make our way up the rock face.

Here, for a start, are several such characters in the opening verses. Each, as it were, is looking up with us at the wall of rock, but from their own angle.

Here are the chief **priests** and elders. For them, the death of Jesus is a political necessity. He has challenged their power, he's captured the crowds' imagination, and he can't be allowed to get away with it. They don't suppose for a minute he might be a true prophet, let alone Israel's **Messiah**. Their naked political goals, unadorned with any desire for true justice, are a constant feature of the story. Do you know anybody like that? Have you ever seen them in the mirror?

Here is a dinner party, the last supper before the Last Supper; and here is an unnamed woman whose love for Jesus has overflowed, quite literally, in an act of needless beauty, like a stunning alpine flower growing unobserved half a mile up a rock face. Of course, some people always want to pick such flowers and make them do something useful – to grow them in a garden at home, perhaps, to make a profit. God's creation isn't like that, and nor is devotion to Jesus. When people start to be captivated by him, and by his path to the cross, the love this produces is given to extravagance. Do you know anybody like that? Do they ever wear your shoes?

Jesus turns aside the grumbles and accepts the devotion. Already he is the central figure, knowing what's coming and beginning to explain what it means, pointing up the long hard climb to the summit itself. Passover, the great festival of freedom, is coming. For the chief priests, the festival simply means a bad time for political assassinations. For Jesus, it's the time of freedom, the time when God will do what he did when he brought the children of Israel out of Egypt. It's the moment when the **covenant** will be renewed, when sins will be forgiven, when God will make a way through the Red Sea, when liberty is bought through the death of the firstborn . . .

And he knows who that firstborn will be, and how it will happen. It will be so swift and sudden that they won't have time to anoint his body properly. The ointment at the Bethany supper party must do instead. The story begins with a sense of urgency. Come quickly. We have a long climb ahead.

MATTHEW 26.14–25

Passover and Betrayal

[14]Then one of the Twelve, called Judas Iscariot, went to the chief priests.

[15]'What will you give me', he said, 'to hand him over to you?'

They agreed on thirty pieces of silver. [16]From that moment on, he was watching for an opportunity to hand him over.

[17]On the first day of the Feast of Unleavened Bread, the disciples said to Jesus, 'Where do you want us to get the Passover ready for you to eat it?'

[18]'Go into the city', he said, 'to a certain man, and say to him, "The Teacher says, 'My time is very close. I'm going to keep the Passover at your house with my disciples.'"'

[19]So the disciples did as Jesus had told them, and got the Passover ready.

[20]When evening came, he settled down with the Twelve. [21]As they were eating, he said, 'I'm telling you the truth: one of you will betray me.' [22]They were extremely upset, and began to say one by one, 'It's not me, is it, Master?'

[23]'It's one who's dipped his hand with me in the dish,' Jesus replied. 'That's the one who will betray me. [24]The son of man is on his way, as the Bible said it would happen, but it's misery for the man who hands him over. It would be better for that man if he'd never been born.'

[25]At this, Judas, who was planning to betray him, said, 'It isn't me, is it, Teacher?'

'You've just said so,' he replied.

'And I thought you were my friend!'

The words were meant to sting, and they did. I looked from one man to the other. The meeting had collapsed into bitter accusations, and this was the final one. The speaker got up from his chair and went over to the window, hiding his tears. The other stayed silent, looking as though he'd just had his face slapped. I was powerless to do or say anything. The chairman quietly suggested we adjourn the meeting, and we all scuttled off gratefully, eager to escape the embarrassment and horror of a shattered relationship.

It's one thing to cheat someone – in business, in politics, in love. It's always ugly and mean. It's always wrong. But betrayal adds a different dimension. It's like setting deceit to music. And the music is always the sort that makes you squirm in your chair, going cross-eyed with the discords and clashes and wondering if it will ever resolve itself.

Well, sometimes it does and sometimes it doesn't. There is something horribly final about betrayal. Oh, it's possible to forgive someone, and of course we are commanded to do so. But forgiveness – going without revenge, continuing to love the person as we love ourselves – doesn't necessarily mean we can ever place the same trust in them again. Would you walk along the branch of a tree that had been sawn through, even if you were told it had been mended? Would you ever again feel at ease with the best friend who had seduced your spouse?

The fact that these very searching human questions are raised here shows what kind of a narrative we are dealing with. The figure of Judas is one of the deepest and darkest not only in the **gospels** but in all literature. People have written whole books trying to get to the bottom of what precisely he did and why. Sometimes he has been used, in much later so-called Christian thinking, as a reason to attack the Jews. His name, after all, is 'Judah', the same root word as 'Judaea'; and in Greek the word for 'Jews' is *Ioudaioi*, 'Judaea-people', 'Judah-people', 'Judas-people'. More recently, some have reacted against this madness in the opposite direction, either suggesting that Judas never existed and that the gospel writers invented him as an anti-Jewish move, or that what he did wasn't betrayal, but part of what Jesus had intended all along.

None of this gets near the heart of the matter. All the characters in the story, except the Roman officials, are of course Jews. And 'Judas', like 'Jesus', was a very common name among first-century Jews. Judah was the patriarch from whose family King David had come; Judas Maccabaeus was the great hero of two centuries before, who had liberated Judaea from the Syrians. The leader of the tax revolt during Jesus' boyhood was called 'Judas the Galilean'. The name had both royal and revolutionary echoes. One of Jesus' own brothers was called Judas. It's not surprising there were two people with that name among the **Twelve** (the other one is probably the same person as 'Thaddaeus' in 10.3).

We constantly have to remind ourselves, in reading this story, that when Jesus said 'one of you will betray me', the other eleven **disciples** didn't at once turn round and point knowingly at Judas. The lists of disciples, like the one in 10.2–4, put him last, and mention the horrible act which has tainted his name from that day to this. But that only shows that the lists were written up later. As far as the other eleven were concerned, he was one of them, sharing their common life, a trusted and valued friend and comrade. He had seen Jesus' wonderful healings. He had heard the **parables**. He had agreed with Peter that Jesus was the **Messiah**. He had come with them into Jerusalem, singing Hosannas, laying his coat on the road, watching in glee as Jesus upset tables, chairs, coins and doves in the **Temple**. He wasn't any different from the rest of them.

But now it had all gone horribly wrong. I suspect that even if we were to transport all we now know of psychology back to the first century, and gain an interview with Judas on the day of the Last Supper, and even if he co-operated and answered all our questions, we still wouldn't get to the bottom of it, to a single identifiable motive that would make us say, 'Of course!

That's why he did it.' Evil isn't like that. It's ultimately absurd. That's part of its danger and darkness.

It wasn't just the money, though that may have helped. If he was going to break ranks with the others, he would need something to help him get started on a different life somewhere else. But the decision to hand Jesus over probably came first. It may have been partly an angry disappointment at the fact that Jesus, having caused such a stir in Jerusalem, was now talking again about going to his death, instead of planning the great moment when he would take over Jerusalem and become king. Maybe Judas had hoped, as James and John had hoped, that he would be Jesus' right-hand man in the new regime. After all, he was the group's treasurer, trusted and valued. Maybe he'd been cherishing all sorts of plans for what he would do when the **kingdom** came. Maybe there was a nice little farm back in Galilee that he'd long had his eye on . . .

Who knows? We certainly don't, and frankly I'm happy not to peer down that murky well for too long. I might see reflections I find disturbing.

But in the middle of the picture once more, almost serene though deeply sad, is Jesus himself, arranging a secret Passover celebration with an unnamed supporter in the city itself, sitting with the Twelve and telling them what was about to happen. The sorrow of his approaching ordeal was overlaid with the sorrow of betrayal. And in that moment we glimpse one element of the meaning of the cross.

Jesus was going to his death wounded by the wounds common to humanity. Greed, lust, ambition: all kinds of natural drives and desires turned in on themselves rather than doing the outward-looking work the creator intended them to. When we say that Jesus died 'because of our sins', we don't just mean that in some high-flown, abstract sense. We mean that what put him on the cross was precisely the sins that we all not only commit but wallow in. 'It isn't me, is it, Master?' Only when you've said that, knowing that it might well be you, can you begin to appreciate what it meant for Jesus to sit at that table and share that Passover meal with them, with Judas too. Or what it means that he has promised to share his feast with us as well.

MATTHEW 26.26–35

The Last Supper

[26]As they were eating, Jesus took some bread, blessed it, broke it and gave it to the disciples.

'Take it and eat it,' he said, 'this is my body.'

[27]Then he took a cup; and, after giving thanks, he gave it to them.

'Drink this, all of you,' he said. [28]'This is my blood of the covenant, which is poured out for many for the forgiveness of sins. [29]But let me tell you this: I will not drink any more from this fruit of the vine, until that day when I drink it new with you in the kingdom of my father.'

[30]They sang a hymn, and went out to the Mount of Olives.

[31]Then Jesus said to them, 'You are all going to stumble and fall tonight because of me. This is what the Bible says, you see:

I shall strike the shepherd,
And the sheep of the flock will be scattered.

[32]'But after I am raised up, I shall go on ahead of you to Galilee.'

[33]'Even if everyone else trips and falls,' said Peter in reply to him, 'I'm never going to do that!'

[34]'I'm telling you the truth,' said Jesus to him, 'this very night, before the cock has crowed, you will deny me three times.'

[35]'Even if I have to die with you,' said Peter to him, 'I won't ever deny you!'

And all the disciples said the same.

There is an article in the newspaper today about two families locked in a highly expensive legal battle. It's all the sadder because they are next-door neighbours.

The case turns on the right of one family to keep on the premises what by most people's standards is a large number of dogs. The dog-owning family are country people, and theirs is a country village. The neighbours have moved from the city, they haven't got animals of their own, and they don't want to be bothered by hearing them and, perhaps, smelling them, all the time.

A trivial example; but it illustrates a phenomenon which is becoming more frequent. City-dwellers have complained, after moving to what seemed like an 'idyllic' country cottage, that the noise of cows and sheep all around is too intrusive for them. And I even heard the other day that someone had grumbled because, having moved to live next door to a farm, the cockerel, or rooster, had an annoying habit of waking them up somewhat earlier in the morning than they had intended. You would have thought people would know that this sort of thing would come with the territory. That's what country living is like.

The story that is about to unfold is the story from which the cockcrow gets the haunting, dark image it has in Western culture. The cock in this story doesn't exactly wake someone up; or maybe that's precisely what it does, rousing Peter from the moral slumber into which he's fallen. Anyone who has walked around Jerusalem in the early morning – particularly in the early morning of Good Friday, commemorating the morning of Jesus' trial before Pilate, and his crucifixion – will know that the sound of the cockcrow, repeated by dozens of roosters in the hours around dawn, sends shivers down the spine as we recall what the same noise, in the same city, meant for Peter two thousand years ago.

The cockcrow, and Peter's denial, are all the more poignant because of what has just happened. Though the **disciples** probably didn't understand it much at the time – it was all too bewildering and unexpected – the meal they shared with Jesus has echoed down the centuries like that insistent cockcrow, reminding us not just of our own failings (though it may do that as well) but of Jesus' coming to meet us, failing as we were, and inviting us to a banquet in which his own self was the food and drink. This is such a strange, and even repellent, idea, that we have to take a couple of steps back from it and approach it with care.

As far as the disciples were concerned, this was a Passover meal. That's what they had prepared. To this day, when Jewish families all over the world celebrate Passover, there is special food and drink, prescribed by custom going back thousands of years. And there are particular words to say.

The words tell the story of how God's people, Israel, came out of Egypt, through the Red Sea, leaving behind their slavery and going on to freedom in their promised land. The food and drink are carefully chosen to symbolize and express aspects of that great event, the **Exodus**. Thus, for instance, there are bitter herbs, which symbolize the hardships the Israelites suffered in Egypt. The head of the household must say the words, introducing the different parts of the meal.

All this, which is so strange to many in the modern world, would have been second nature to the disciples. They would of course have been expecting Jesus to take the part of the leader in this regular, annual celebration of God's promised freedom.

And so he did. But, in doing so, he drew the meaning of the whole meal on to himself. He offered a new direction of thought which, for those who followed him and came to believe in him, took Passover in quite a new direction, which has likewise continued to this day. We can perhaps imagine the shock of the disciples as they realized he was departing from the normal script and talking about . . . *himself*.

'My body, my very self . . . here it is!'

155

'My blood, my life, my death, all for you, all so that sins can be forgiven . . . here it is!'

Look around the room in your mind's eye and see the reaction. Peter, furious that Jesus is still talking about dying, and on such a special evening as well. Thomas, giving a little shake of the head. He'd not understood more than a third of what had gone before, and he doesn't understand this at all. John (if indeed it is John, reclining close to Jesus) looking up in astonishment, in a mixture of love and fear. Judas (Matthew implies that he's still here at this point) frozen in his place, wondering how much Jesus knows and how much he's guessed.

And you? What is your reaction to this extraordinary performance?

For many Christians, the regular celebration in which we copy Jesus, remembering that Last Supper and repeating its action in order to go back in heart and mind to the original setting, and nourish ourselves once more with the death and life and presence and *personality* of Jesus – for many of us, this is a central part of our story. We couldn't do without it. But for other Christians, it has remained a puzzle, a bit threatening, perhaps. It's been so overlaid with different meanings, and seems to have caused so many squabbles, that people are almost shy about it.

The heart of the matter is reasonably straightforward, though none the less breathtaking. Jesus was drawing into one event a millennium and more of Jewish celebrations. The Jews had believed for some while that the original Exodus pointed on to a new one, in which God would do at last what he had long promised: he would forgive the sins of Israel and the world, once and for all. Sin, a far greater slave-master than Egypt had ever been, would be defeated in the way God defeated not only Egypt but also the Red Sea. And now Jesus, sitting there at a secret meal in Jerusalem, was saying, by what he was doing as much as by the words he was speaking: this is the moment. This is the time. And it's all because of what's going to happen to me.

Jesus' action at the Last Supper was, you see, the equivalent in symbolic language (and symbols are the most powerful form of communication) of those sayings about the **son of man** being handed over, and giving his life as a ransom for many (20.28). Somehow, identifying the bread and the wine with his body (about to be broken in death) and his blood (about to be spilt on the cross), and inviting his followers to share it and find in it the gift of forgiveness of sins, of new life, of God's **kingdom** – somehow this action had then, and still has today, a power beyond words. A power to touch and heal parts of our broken and messy lives. A power to tell the world around that Jesus is Lord (see 1 Corinthians 11.26).

But, perhaps because that power always remains mysterious, and never in our own control, many people found then and find still that it's all too much. The disciples, instead of being heartened and encouraged, were all about to be scattered, as Jesus went alone to face the darkest night of the world. Peter, big, strong, blustering Peter, was about to be reduced to a spluttering, lying, weeping fool. Perhaps that tells us something, too, about the power of Jesus' action. Perhaps when it starts to have its effect the first sign is that we learn just how weak and needy we are. Perhaps the combination of Last Supper and cockcrow will always haunt us, always challenge us, always lay bare our continuing need for God's redeeming love, until the new day dawns and Jesus shares with us the new wine of the kingdom of God.

MATTHEW 26.36–46

Gethsemane

[36]So Jesus went with them to the place called Gethsemane.
'You sit here,' he said to the disciples, 'while I go over there

and pray.'

[37]He took Peter and the two sons of Zebedee with him, and began to be very upset and distressed.

[38]'My soul is overwhelmed with grief,' he said, 'even to death. Stay here and keep watch with me.'

[39]Then, going a little further on, he fell on his face and prayed.

'My father,' he said, 'if it's possible – please, please let this cup go away from me! But . . . not what I want, but what you want.'

[40]He came back to the disciples and found them asleep.

'So,' he said to Peter, 'couldn't you keep watch with me for a single hour? [41]Watch and pray so that you don't get pulled down into the time of testing. The spirit is eager, but the body is weak.'

[42]Again, for the second time, he went off and said, 'My father, if it's not possible for this to pass unless I drink it, let your will be done.'

[43]Again he came and found them asleep; their eyes were heavy. [44]Once more he left them and went away. He prayed for the third time, using the same words once again. [45]Then he came back to the disciples.

'You can sleep now,' he said, 'and have a good rest! Look – the time has come, and the son of man is given over over into the hands of wicked people! [46]Get up and let's be going. Look! Here comes the one who's going to betray me!'

There was once a small girl who had never seen her father anything but cheerful.

As long as she could remember, he seemed to have been smiling at her. He had smiled when she was born, the daughter he had longed for. He had smiled as he held her in his arms and helped her to learn to eat and drink. He had laughed as he played with her, encouraged her with games and toys as she learned to walk, chatted brightly as he took her to school. If she hurt herself, his smile and gentle kiss helped her to relax and get over it. If she was in difficulties or trouble, the shadow that would cross his face was like a small cloud which hardly succeeded in hiding the sun; soon the smile would come out again, the eager interest in some new project, something to distract, to move on to new worlds.

And then one day it happened.

To begin with she wasn't told why. He came back home from a visit, and with a look she'd never seen before went straight to his room. Ever afterwards she would remember the sounds she then heard, the sounds she never thought to hear.

The sound of a healthy, strapping 30-year-old man weeping for a dead sister.

It was of course a necessary part of growing up. In most families, grief would have struck sooner. Looking back, she remained grateful for the years when smiles and laughter were all she could remember. But the shock of his sudden vulnerability, far more than the fact of the death of her aunt and all that it meant, were what made the deepest impression.

I think Gethsemane was the equivalent moment for the **disciples**.

Oh, Jesus had been sad at various times. He'd been frustrated with them for not understanding what he was talking about. He'd been cross with the people who were attacking him, misunderstanding him, accusing him of all sorts of ridiculous things. There had even been tension with his own family. But basically he'd always been the strong one. Always ready with another story, another sharp one-liner to turn the tables on some probing questioner, another soaring vision of God and the **kingdom**. It was always they who had the problems, he who had the answers.

And now this.

Jesus was like a man in a waking nightmare. He could see, as though it was before his very eyes, the cup. Not the cup he had spoken of, and given them to drink, in the intense and exciting atmosphere of the Last Supper an hour or so before. This was the cup he had mentioned to James and John (20.22–23), the cup the prophets had spoken of. The cup of God's wrath.

He didn't want to drink it. He badly didn't want to. Jesus at this point was no hero-figure, marching boldly towards his oncoming fate. He was no Socrates, drinking the poison and telling his friends to stop crying because he was going to a much better life. He was a man, as we might say, in melt-down mode. He had looked into the darkness and seen the grinning faces of all the **demons** in the world looking back at him. And he begged and begged his father not to bring him to the point of going through with it. He prayed the prayer he had taught them to pray: Don't let us be brought into the time of testing, the time of deepest trial!

And the answer was No.

Actually, we can see the answer being given, more subtly than that implies, as the first frantic and panicky prayer turns into the second and then the third. To begin with, a straight request ('Let the cup pass me by'), with a sad recognition that God has the right to say 'No' if that's the way it has to be. Then, a prayer which echoes another phrase in the Lord's Prayer: if it has to be, 'may your will be done'. The disciples probably didn't realize that, when Jesus gave them the Lord's Prayer (6.9–13), this much of it would be so directly relevant to him. He had to live what he taught. Indeed, the whole Sermon on the Mount seemed to be coming true in him, as he himself faced the suffering and sorrow of which he'd spoken, on his way to being struck on the cheek, to being cursed and responding with blessings. Here, for the second time in the **gospel** narrative (the first time being the temptation story in 4.1–11), we see Jesus fighting in private the spiritual battle he needed to win if he was then to stand in public and speak, and live, and die for God's kingdom.

The shocking lesson for the disciples can, of course, be turned to excellent use if we learn, in our own prayer, to wait with them, to keep awake and watch with Jesus. At any given moment, someone we know is facing darkness and horror: illness, death, bereavement, torture, catastrophe, loss. They ask us, perhaps silently, to stay with them, to watch and pray alongside them.

Distance is no object. In any one day we may be called to kneel in Gethsemane beside someone dying in a hospital in Nairobi, someone being tortured for their **faith** in Burma, someone who has lost a job in New York, someone else waiting anxiously for a doctor's report in Edinburgh. Once we ourselves get over the shock of realizing that all our friends, neighbours and family, and even the people we have come to rely on, are themselves vulnerable and need our support – if even Jesus longed for his friends' support, how much more should we! – we should be prepared to give it to the fullest of our ability.

And when we ourselves find the ground giving way beneath our feet, as sooner or later we shall, Gethsemane is where to go. That is where we find that the Lord of the world, the one to whom is now committed all authority (28.18), has been there before us.

MATTHEW 26.47–56

Jesus is Arrested

⁴⁷While Jesus was still speaking, there was Judas, one of the Twelve! He had come with a large crowd, with swords and clubs, from the chief priests and the elders of the people. ⁴⁸The one who was intending to betray him gave them a sign: 'The one I kiss – that's him! Grab hold of him!'

⁴⁹So he went up at once to Jesus and said 'Greetings, Teacher!', and kissed him.

⁵⁰'My friend,' said Jesus, 'what are you doing here?'

Then they came and laid hands on Jesus, and arrested him.

⁵¹At that, one of the men with Jesus reached out his hand, drew his sword and hit the high priest's slave, cutting off his ear.

⁵²'Put your sword back where it belongs!' said Jesus to him. 'People who use the sword die by the sword! ⁵³Don't you realize that I could call on my father and have him send me more than twelve legions of angels, just like that? ⁵⁴But how then can the Bible come true when it says this has to happen?'

⁵⁵At that time Jesus said to the crowds, 'Have you really come out with swords and sticks to arrest me, as if I were some kind of brigand? I sat there teaching in the Temple every day, and you didn't arrest me! ⁵⁶But all this has happened so that what the prophets said in the Bible would be fulfilled.'

Then all the disciples abandoned him and ran away.

A radio station telephoned me, and before I knew what was happening I found myself talking, live, to a large and invisible audience. A leading Muslim writer in Britain had been urging the Government to tighten up the blasphemy laws – the laws that prohibit people from saying rude things about religions or their leading figures (such as Muhammad, or Jesus). Other voices were saying that people should have the freedom to say what they wanted, whenever they wanted, about anyone or anything. Censorship, after all, is regarded by many people in the West as being in itself worse than anything the censors could want to ban.

I confess that until that telephone call I had not really given the matter very much thought. But as soon as the question came to me ('Did I think we needed to tighten the laws that stop people saying rude things about Jesus?'), I knew where to turn for an answer. I turned to the **disciple** with the sword in the garden.

Now of course there is more to the question than meets the

eye. When many families and groups move from a country where their religion is in a majority, and begin a new life in a country where they are in a small minority, they will have many reasons for feeling insecure. If, in that setting, people in the host community start saying rude things about their religion, they may be right to think that this is part of a desire to reject them as members of the community. If, however, an apparent majority religion tries to prevent any criticism or negative comments, it looks as though it's using its power for its own ends. Wide-ranging laws can be very blunt instruments, and it's always important to protect the weak and vulnerable.

But when someone swung a sword around in among the olive trees in dark Gethsemane, thinking it was his God-given duty to defend Jesus, Jesus told him not to bother. In fact, he told him he was heading for disaster. People who live by the sword tend to die by the sword. Jesus was about to face a whole long evening of insults, torture, mocking, spitting, cursing and shaming, and except for a few quite calm words he remained silent. Had any of his followers been present and offered to defend him he would certainly have said to them what he said in the garden.

What this means for the laws of nations today, I can't say. I emphasize again that all nations have a responsibility to care for the weak, for those who face danger or prejudice for whatever reason. There is a lesser obligation to prevent people doing things that others happen to find offensive. In the multi-cultural societies that many of us live in today, it's by no means easy to decide where to draw those lines. But we have to face the fact that, from the very first, people found Jesus himself offensive. Their reaction to him, however much we may think it unwarranted, is at the root of their reaction, often, to his followers today.

Consider how the evening's events played out. The crowd that came to arrest Jesus brought swords and clubs. Jesus was certainly justified in teasing them for treating him as though he was a heavily armed brigand with a band of soldiers to protect him. However, they knew he was talking about God's **kingdom**, and doing some powerful things to back it up. They may have figured that they could take no chances. If they were going to do anything during Passover-time, it had to be quickly, at night, away from the huge crowds that were filling the city. (Gethsemane is just outside the city walls, down a steep hill to the east of the **Temple** mount, at the foot of the Mount of Olives which goes steeply up the other side of the Kidron valley.) What Jesus had been saying and doing was not perceived as what we mean by 'religious'. If you talked about God's kingdom at Passover-time, it could never be merely a matter of private spirituality. It meant revolution. If someone else had a rival plan, it meant violence. If they caught you, it probably meant death.

We have already spoken of the motives of Judas, or rather of the difficulty in fathoming what they were (26.14–16, 21–25). Now we see, with overwhelming pathos, Jesus' last reaction to the traitor as he led the arresting party right to the place where he knew they would find him. 'My friend,' he says, 'what are you doing here?' (Or possibly, 'do what you've come to do'; the words in the original are a bit cryptic, but I think it's more likely that Jesus was posing a last gentle question to Judas: Do you really want to go through with this?) It is of course the word 'friend' that causes us to catch our breath. Friendship, for Jesus, does not stop with betrayal, even though now it is tinged with deep sadness.

But what stands out most from this picture is the strong sense which Jesus had that he was taking part in a real-life play for which the script had been written – if only one could decode it properly – in the Bible, centuries before. The prophets and other writers had spoken of the way in which God's saving plan for Israel would pass through a dark night of suffering and even death, before bursting out into the glorious new day of God's kingdom. Jesus had lived all his life in conscious obedience to what he took to be the biblical drama, intending to be the one who would bring it to fulfilment.

Matthew, as always, is himself on the lookout for this theme of biblical fulfilment. But he didn't invent it. If we want to understand what made Jesus himself do and say what he did and said, and what he believed was to happen to him and what it would mean, the only place to look is in the biblical stories and prophecies he knew and lived on. And there we find the strange picture of the shepherd who would suffer, the cup that would be drunk, the servant who would die for sinners, the **son of man** who would be vindicated after his suffering. Jesus' agonizing prayer in Gethsemane has rooted him once more in his own biblically based vocation. That's what prayer often does.

MATTHEW 26.57–68

Jesus Before Caiaphas

[57]The people who had arrested Jesus took him off to Caiaphas the high priest. The scribes and elders had already gathered at his house. [58]Peter, however, followed him at some distance, all the way to the high priest's residence. He went in and sat with the servants, to see how things would work out.

[59]The high priest and the whole Council tried to produce false evidence against Jesus, to frame a capital charge and have him killed. [60]But even though they brought in plenty of lying witnesses, they couldn't find the evidence they wanted. Finally two people came forward [61]and declared:

'This fellow said, "I can destroy God's Temple and build it again in three days!"'

[62]Then the high priest stood up.

'Aren't you going to answer?' he said to him. 'What are these people accusing you of?'

[63]But Jesus remained silent.

Then the high priest said to him,

'I put you on oath before the living God: tell us if you are the Messiah, God's son!'

[64]'You said the words,' replied Jesus. 'But let me tell you this: from now on you will see "the son of man sitting at the right hand of Power, and coming on the clouds of heaven".'

[65]Then the high priest tore his robes.

'He's blasphemed!' he said. 'Why do we need any more witnesses? Look – you've heard his blasphemy, here and now! [66]What's your verdict?'

'He deserves to die,' they answered.

[67]Then they spat in his face and hit him. Some of them slapped him, [68]and said, 'Prophesy for us, Mr Messiah! Who was it who hit you?'

Have you ever watched two people speaking to each other in different languages, neither understanding the other?

Sometimes it's funny, and effective. I remember watching with surprise and delight as my daughter, aged about five, played on holiday with a little girl of a similar age, the one speaking English, the other French. Neither understood a word the other was saying. It's remarkable how far you can get with body language, tone of voice, and a shared sand-box.

Sometimes it's very threatening. I once watched in alarm as two motorists shouted at each other after a minor traffic accident which threatened, or so it seemed at the time, to become a major international incident. Both were assuming that the other understood, and were shouting louder in their own languages (German and Italian, I think) as though that would get their point across. I left them to it.

And now we watch as Jesus and Caiaphas seem to be playing the same kind of game. Only it isn't a game, and it's not just an international incident. It is two world-views coming face to face in a dramatic showdown after eyeing one another at a distance for some while. And with the world-views went different languages – not different actual languages, of course, since both were presumably speaking Aramaic, but different ways of seeing and describing the whole world, giving birth to two different, and mutually incomprehensible, ways of talking.

The central question at issue shows what I mean. The question was about the **Temple**, and about messiahship.

Caiaphas knew that Jesus had been leading a **kingdom-of-God** movement, and that he had done some strange things, not least in Jerusalem itself. It seemed that he was laying claim to some kind of authority over the Temple. But Caiaphas lived in a world where he, as **high priest**, had supreme authority over the Temple. He lived in a world where he, as high priest, had received God's anointing (remember that '**Messiah**' means literally 'the anointed one'). He must have known that there were debates about whether, in the end, God's coming king would displace the priesthood, or whether king and priest would stand side by side; but he probably didn't bother much about theoretical questions. What mattered were the practical matters: keeping the peace with Rome, keeping the mob happy, keeping trouble-makers well away from Jerusalem, especially around Passover-time. The world of *realpolitik* was the world where his language made whatever sense it did.

Jesus, however, lived in a different world. He had been going around Galilee and Judaea doing and saying things whose clear implication was that God was doing a new thing; a new thing, moreover, that would upstage the Temple itself. Wherever he was, folk discovered that it was like being in the Temple for a great festival. People got healed, people were celebrating, people even found forgiveness of sins, found the love and presence of God, which they'd assumed they'd only find in the Temple or by studying **Torah**. They didn't have to go and get it. It was coming to meet them and embrace them.

Jesus lived in that world and it sprang to life around him.

He had indeed said that the Temple would be destroyed, but not that he would do it himself. Presumably the 'false witnesses' had got hold of a garbled report of something like 24.2, or John 2.19. But the reason for this warning was because he could see that the Temple had come to represent the wrong turn that many in Israel, not least the leadership, had taken, away from God's calling to be the light of the world and down the dark road of rebellion.

Realizing the radical difference between his world and that of Caiaphas, and the impossibility of explaining what he was doing and saying in words that Caiaphas would understand, Jesus remained silent. Until, that is, the high priest, anxious to secure some kind of quasi-legal conviction that he could take to the Roman governor the next day, put him on oath. Then, and only then, Jesus speaks; but he speaks in his own language, the language he has learned and lived for many years: the language of biblical prophecy.

His answer to the question of messiahship is the same oblique form of 'Yes' that he gave to Judas in 26.25: 'You've just said so,' or 'those are your words'. It was perhaps a way of avoiding arrogance or apparent selfish pride. But the ringing affirmation which followed made it quite clear that Jesus saw himself and his work in terms of the biblical picture of messiahship (the passage about the **son of man** in Daniel 7, quoted here, was sometimes taken messianically at that time). What's more, he saw the confrontation between himself and Caiaphas as the concrete outworking of the clash between that 'son of man' and the Fourth Beast (Daniel 7.7–8), the monster that was waging war against the true representative of God's people.

The two languages belonged in worlds that were not only incompatible and mutually incomprehensible; they were bound to meet in head-on collision. God would vindicate one or the other. Jesus staked his life on the belief that God would vindicate him. That is what the quotation from Daniel 7 means, as we saw in 24.30. And Jesus coupled his claim with an echo of Psalm 110.1: the Messiah will be seated at God's right hand. It was hardly surprising that Caiaphas saw this as blasphemy.

From here events could take their course. Caiaphas could present the crowds with the charge of blasphemy, to explain to them that Jesus had been an impostor, a deceiver, leading Israel astray. To the Romans, he could say that Jesus was a would-be Messiah, in other words, a rebel king. The court, breaking up for the night in disarray, lost no time in showing Jesus what they thought of his claim.

Underneath the highly charged meeting of high priest and Messiah, the dark question remains. How do you speak God's truth into a situation where lies and distortion, injustice and ambition, have created a world in which words mean different things? How can the church, faced with social, political, cultural and religious settings which have generated their own new language, continue to speak truthfully of Jesus? Those who have tried to speak the truth in dangerous situations will know that people seem almost bound to misunderstand them. How can individual Christians remain loyal to Jesus, knowing when to keep silent and when to speak in such a way that true wisdom may be heard?

MATTHEW 26.69–75

Peter's Denial

[69]Meanwhile, Peter sat outside in the courtyard.

One of the servant-girls came up to him. 'You were with Jesus the Galilean too, weren't you?' she said.

[70]He denied it in front of everyone.

'I don't know what you're talking about,' he said.

[71]He went out to the gateway. Another girl saw him, and said to the people who were there, 'This fellow was with Jesus the Nazarene!'

⁷²Once more he denied it, this time swearing, 'I don't know the man!'

⁷³After a little while the people standing around came up and said to Peter, 'You really are one of them! Look – the way you talk makes it obvious!'

⁷⁴Then he began to curse and swear, 'I don't know the man!' And then, all at once, the cock crowed.

⁷⁵And Peter remembered.

He remembered the words Jesus had spoken to him: 'Before the cock crows, you will deny me three times.'

And he went outside and cried like a baby.

In his novel *Thinks...*, the English writer David Lodge tells the story of a woman who discovers, after his death, that her husband, whom she had loved and trusted, had been regularly unfaithful to her for several years. At the same time, she meets an unscrupulous computer scientist, who tries to persuade her, among other things, that computers can, in principle, do the things that humans can do, including thinking for themselves. She resists this idea, but with difficulty and without total conviction.

Meanwhile, she has built up a deep anger and resentment against her late husband. Finally, returning to her old home towards the end of the book, and seeing his photographs, something in her gives way; and she breaks down and cries and cries. And she forgives him.

And then she realizes the answer to the other question: this is something a computer could never, ever do. 'Crying', she says, 'is a puzzler.' It seems to come from somewhere which works closely in harmony with the bits of us that computers can replicate, and yet it goes so far beyond what they can do that we have to see tears as a key signpost of what it means to be a human being.

Peter's tears at the end of this story are the main thing that distinguish him from Judas in the next chapter. There is all the difference in the world between genuine **repentance** and mere remorse, as Paul wryly notes in one of his letters to Corinth (2 Corinthians 7.10). The one leads to life, the other to death. Peter's tears, shaming, humiliating and devastating though they were, were a sign of life. Judas's anger and bitterness led straight to death.

They had been a long time coming. Peter had recovered quite quickly, we may imagine, from the near-humiliation of trying to walk on the water only to need rescuing (14.28–31). He had, no doubt, been hurt and humiliated when Jesus spun round and told him off, telling him he was a **satan** (16.23). He had been perplexed with the rest of them as Jesus had done dramatic things in Jerusalem and then had failed (as it must have seemed) to capitalize on them, continuing instead with his apparent determination to walk straight into a trap. Peter had done his best in the garden, as he said he would; but his best hadn't been good enough, and he must have had a sense that he'd both let Jesus down by not defending him and let him down in another way by trying to do so in the wrong way.

And now this. Tired, frightened, short on sleep but long on wine from the meal earlier. Doing the right thing (following Jesus) for the wrong reason (wounded pride). Or perhaps, depending how you look at it, the wrong thing (walking straight into a trap, despite Jesus warning them against the time of trial) for the right reason (dogged loyalty). Who knows, or cares? The muddled motives and mixed emotions were no match for the three little questions, from a couple of serving-girls and a courtier with an ear for a northern accent. They were like small pins stuck into a large balloon, and Peter's world exploded in a roar of oaths and a flood of bitter tears.

Denying Jesus is such a sad thing to do. And yet we all do it. Despite the differences of culture and situation, we can even notice parallels, so close as to be almost amusing, between where Peter was that night and where we may find ourselves.

171

A good dinner, plenty of wine. Lots of excitement. Short on sleep but determined to stay in the action. Then a few questions from people we don't even know.

'You're not one of those Jesus-freaks, are you?'

'I mean, nobody here actually *believes* in Jesus, do they?'

'Well, it's all right to be interested in Jesus, but you don't want to take it to extremes, do you?'

Or perhaps it's more subtle. Where frontal attack fails, the enemy will sneak round to an unlocked side entrance.

'If I don't make it in tomorrow, you will sign the office list for me to say I was there, won't you?'

'Go on – it's just this once and nobody will know.'

'You don't mind making a little bit on the side, do you?'

It speaks volumes both for the accuracy of the **gospels** and the humility of the leaders in the early church that Peter's story, in all its graphic detail, remains there starkly in all four gospels. Of course, it makes other points as well: notably, that Jesus, who told him he'd do it, was a true prophet despite what Caiaphas and the others thought. But probably the main reason for this story being told and retold was simply that it provided such an excellent example of how not to do it. The early church was full of people who started off enthusiastically and then ran the risk of losing steam halfway down the line. Today's church faces the same problem.

Equally, the early church saw many people, both great leaders and insignificant serving-girls (not that anyone is insignificant in God's family), stand up to questioning, persecution, torture and death rather than deny Jesus. If Peter could have seen young and innocent Christians, 200 years later, facing lions in the amphitheatre rather than deny their Lord, he would perhaps have felt that his negative example had served some purpose. What would he think if he could see the church today?

MATTHEW 27.1–10

The Death of Judas

¹When dawn broke, all the chief priests and elders of the people held a council meeting about Jesus, in order to have him put to death. ²They tied him up, took him off, and handed him over to Pilate, the governor.

³Meanwhile Judas, who had betrayed him, saw that he had been condemned, and was filled with remorse. He took the thirty pieces of silver back to the high priests and elders.

⁴'I've sinned!' he said. 'I betrayed an innocent man, and now I've got his blood on my hands!'

'See if we care!' they replied. 'It's your problem.'

⁵And he threw down the money in the Temple, and left, and went and hanged himself.

⁶'Well now,' said the chief priests, picking up the money. 'According to the law, we can't put it into the Temple treasury, because it's got blood on it.'

⁷So they had a discussion, and used it to buy the Potter's Field, as a burial place for foreigners. ⁸(That's why that field is called Blood Field, to this day.) ⁹Then the word that was spoken by Jeremiah the prophet came true:

They took the thirty pieces of silver,
the price of the one who was valued,
valued by the children of Israel;
¹⁰and they gave them for the potter's field,
as the Lord instructed me.

Perhaps the most interesting thing about this story is the people who do *not* show remorse.

In many countries, a feature of the criminal justice system is that people who have been jailed for serious crimes often become eligible for parole, or possibly even for early release, if they show genuine remorse for what they have done. The system breaks down, of course, when someone who was wrongfully imprisoned refuses to show remorse for a crime he or she didn't commit, and so stays in prison years longer than if they had agreed to play along with the false verdict. But at least several justice systems do try to acknowledge the importance of facing up to the consequences of one's actions.

But there are levels, and degrees, of remorse. We saw when we looked at Peter, at the end of the previous chapter, that there is a big difference between remorse, such as that of Judas, and genuine **repentance**, such as that of Peter. There is a watershed between them. Like drops of rain falling near a mountain-top, they may start quite close together, but depending which side of the line they fall they will make their way to one side of the country or the other. Rain to the east of Jerusalem (very rare, by the way) will flow down to the Dead Sea; rain to the west will go into the Mediterranean. Remorse and repentance both begin with looking at something you've done and realizing it was wrong. But the first goes down the hill of anger, recrimination, self-hatred and ultimately self-destruction, the way that leads to death. The second goes down the route Peter took, of tears, shame, and a way back to life.

The chief **priests** and elders showed no remorse for their night's work. As far as they were concerned, they had done their duty to God and their country. Whether Jesus was guilty or innocent was supremely indifferent to them. What mattered was that he was causing an uproar, making trouble, risking calling down the anger of Rome. The chief priests, as we'll see, weren't exactly on excellent terms with Rome, nor was the Roman governor particularly keen on them. But Rome meant trouble, and trouble was best kept at bay. Or, to put it another way, if the eagles want carrion to gnaw on, let's throw them another failed **Messiah** and maybe they'll not worry about the rest of us.

The result was that when a man came into the **Temple** complaining bitterly of guilt, pleading for some kind of help, none was forthcoming. We shouldn't miss the irony. This isn't just about Judas wishing he'd never been born and the priests remaining aloof. This is the beginning of the end for the Temple.

The house has after all been built on the sand, and will fall with a crash. Jesus has said to the Temple mountain, 'Be cast into the sea', and it's getting ready to go. The Messiah has turned over the tables – he has stopped the sacrifices for a few brief but significant moments – and now the Temple authorities themselves can't help a man who complains of guilt and impurity. The chief priest has refused to listen to the Messiah's warnings and challenges, and the whole system he represents is starting to crumble.

The tragedy of Judas is real, horrible and lasting. But the tragedy of the Temple is worse. And its official custodians are so busy looking after their own political interests that they can't see the foundations sinking into the sand, and the tell-tale cracks in the masonry.

Do we have here, I wonder, a further insight into what poor, muddled Judas thought he was doing? Why did he only show remorse when Jesus was condemned to death? Did he think that maybe, if he engineered a confrontation between Jesus and Caiaphas, Jesus would give Caiaphas such a devastating answer that everyone would be convinced? Or did he hope that Jesus would then decide it was time to summon the twelve legions of angels he had on call if needed? That doesn't explain the thirty pieces of silver. But then, as we said before, evil is not always consistent or rational.

Meanwhile, Jesus is on his way to the governor.

From sources outside the New Testament (mostly the historian Josephus), we know, comparatively speaking, quite a lot about Pontius Pilate. He was a minor Roman official a long way from home, who was frequently accused by his subjects of heavy-handed or ill-considered judgments. He got into trouble for one or two major mistakes. He allowed troops to kill innocent and unarmed civilians. He used money from the Temple treasury for secular purposes (building an aqueduct). He ruled Judaea for ten years (AD 26–36), and when he was eventually recalled in disgrace no tears were shed in the Middle East.

This is the man before whom Jesus will now stand, the Jesus to whom Matthew has introduced us during the course of his **gospel**. The meeting of Jesus and Caiaphas saw a clash of worlds and a failure of communication. The meeting of Jesus of Nazareth and Pontius Pilate is the closest the story comes to a showdown between **Christ** and Caesar, between the King of the Jews and the (self-acclaimed) Lord of the world. And, as both sides use the weapons that match their particular type of claim, we, the gospel readers, are invited to watch in awe to see which of the two – the power of aggression, translated into a 'justice' system designed to suit the rulers, or the power of silence, suffering and love – is in fact vindicated by God. That is a major part of what the gospel writers are trying to tell us about the meaning of the cross.

MATTHEW 27.11–26

Jesus and Barabbas Before Pilate

[11]So Jesus stood in front of the governor.

'Are you the King of the Jews?' the governor asked him.

'If you say so,' replied Jesus.

[12]The chief priests and elders poured out their accusations against him, but he made no answer.

[13]Then Pilate said to him, 'Don't you hear all this evidence they're bringing against you?'

[14]He gave him no answer, not even a word, which quite astonished the governor.

[15]Now the governor had a custom. At festival-time he used to release one prisoner for the crowd, whoever they chose.

[16]Just then they had a famous prisoner, called Jesus Barabbas. [17]So when the people were all gathered there, Pilate said to them,

'Who do you want me to release for you? Jesus Barabbas, or Jesus the so-called Messiah?' [18](He knew that they'd handed him over out of sheer envy.)

[19]While he was presiding in the court, his wife sent a message to him.

'Don't have anything to do with that man,' she said. 'He's innocent! I've had a really bad time today in a dream, all because of him.'

[20]The high priests and the elders persuaded the crowds to ask for Barabbas, and to have Jesus killed. [21]So when the governor came back to them again, and asked, 'Which of the two do you want me to release for you?' they said, 'Barabbas!'

[22]'So what shall I do with Jesus the so-called Messiah?' asked Pilate.

'Let him be crucified!' they all said.

[23]'Why?' asked Pilate. 'What's he done wrong?'

But they shouted all the louder, 'Let him be crucified!'

[24]Pilate saw that it was no good. In fact, there was a riot brewing. So he took some water and washed his hands in front of the crowd.

'I'm not guilty of this man's blood,' he said. 'It's your problem.'

[25]'Let his blood be on us!' answered all the people, 'and on our children!'

[26]Then Pilate released Barabbas for them. He had Jesus flogged, and handed him over to be crucified.

One of the most dramatic scenes in Charles Dickens' novels comes at the end of *A Tale of Two Cities*. Set in the French Revolution, the novel's central figure is one Sydney Carton, a man who has done nothing very good with his life, and much that is, to put it mildly, less than good. As the novel reaches its climax, the aristocracy are being sent in droves to the guillotine. Carton, observing, sees a chance to make something of his life, to do something worthwhile, to grow in moral stature in a way he has never done before, to give his family something to be proud of when they remember him. He takes the place of a French aristocrat who is about to be executed. He goes to the guillotine himself and sets another man free. It is, as he says, a far, far better thing to do than he has ever done.

I remember the story well because I first met it, in a televised adaptation, when I was really too young to watch something as frightening as that. (It was my first introduction to Dickens, to guillotines, and for that matter to the French Revolution.) But of course part of the power of the story comes from the fact that it draws on an older tale woven deep into the consciousness of all cultures where the **gospel** of Jesus has penetrated. As the story of Jesus' crucifixion winds towards its great climax, pulling more and more characters and motives into its wake, there now emerges into the light one who summed up, in the most unlikely way, one of its central themes. When Jesus dies, Barabbas goes free.

That was not Pilate's intention. It was not, in that form, anybody's intention. It was part of the strange fate of the moment, that there should be, in prison in Jerusalem, a notorious brigand leader who (like several other rebel leaders of the time) bore the common name Jesus. 'Jesus Barabbas', he was called, and Matthew rubs our noses in the fact of Pilate asking the crowd to choose, for their festival celebration, one of these Jesuses to be released. We are, perhaps, not likely to miss the point Matthew wants to make, but he presses on. By the end of the passage it is crystal clear. Barabbas represents all of us. When Jesus dies, the brigand goes free, the sinners go free, we all go free. That, after all, is what a Passover story ought to be about.

The subtlety was completely lost on Pilate. The only subtle point he wanted to make in this whole sorry tale was that he wasn't guilty. It wasn't his fault. Some people have thought the gospel writers were sympathetic to Pilate, but that's quite wrong. They are as scornful of him as the Jews of the time were resentful. Pilate commanded troops. He had sent them to quell riots before and could do so again. He didn't have to be pushed around. But, like all bullies, he was also a coward. He lurches from trying to play the high and mighty judge to listening a little too much to the growing noise of the crowd.

When Pilate washes his hands, Matthew doesn't think for a moment that he is any the less guilty. The point is not that guilt is in fact transferred to the crowd, and to their children – the children who would grow up as the next generation of brigands, to be cut down or crucified in their thousands by Pilate's heirs and successors as Jerusalem lurched towards its final downfall in AD 70. The point for Matthew is that *all* are guilty: the chief **priests** and elders who have handed Jesus over; Pilate the weak bully; and the crowds themselves. And part of the reason for stressing universal guilt is that, with the death of Jesus, redemption is offered to all. What happened, close up and in sharp focus, to Barabbas is now open to all. When Jesus dies as King of the Jews, he draws on to himself the guilt and death of Israel, and thence also of the world.

All the time there are voices whispering, 'He's innocent! He's innocent!' Pilate's wife sends him a message, picking up intuitively that there is something deeply wrong about sending this man to his death. (Throughout this story it is the women who speak or act truly: the unnamed woman who anointed Jesus, the servant-girls who challenge Peter's concealment, the women at the cross and beside the tomb.) 'He's innocent,' she says, and Pilate knows in his bones both that she's right and that he's not going to take any notice.

But Jesus' innocence is the key to Matthew's meaning. Had he been another rabble-rouser, another Barabbas, what would be gained by swapping one such for another? There is guilt and shame all around: Peter and Judas are now left behind, the chief priests and other leaders have done their worst, the crowds have cheerfully implicated themselves, and now the Roman administration shows what sort of a thing its much-prized 'justice' really was, coming in for its own load both of guilt and of stomach-turning hypocrisy. The human systems that carve up the world between them conspired to put Jesus on the cross. But his innocence of the charges laid against him is the clue to the meaning that Matthew wants us to find there. Jesus dies in the place of the sinner. His great Passover action makes a way through the Red Sea of sin and death, inviting Barabbas, and an increasing multitude ever since, to walk through to freedom.

MATTHEW 27.27–38

Jesus Mocked and Crucified

27Then the soldiers of the governor took Jesus into the barracks, and gathered the whole regiment together. 28They took off his clothes and dressed him up in a scarlet military cloak. 29They wove a crown out of thorns and stuck it on his head, and put a reed in his right hand. Then they knelt down in front of him.

'Greetings, King of the Jews!' they said, making fun of him.

30They spat on him. Then they took the reed and beat him about the head. 31When they had finished mocking him, they took off the cloak, dressed him in his own clothes again, and led him off to crucify him.

32As they were going out they found a man from Cyrene, called Simon. They forced him to carry his cross.

33When they came to the place called Golgotha, which means Skull-Place, 34they gave him a drink of wine mixed with bitter herbs. When he tasted it, he refused to drink it.

35So they crucified him. They divided up his clothes by casting lots, 36and they sat down and kept watch over him there. 37And they placed the written charge above his head: 'This is Jesus, the King of the Jews.'

³⁸Then they crucified two brigands alongside him, one on his right and one on his left.

Almost the whole world is now a tourist trap. Countries compete with each other to attract visitors, particularly from the richer parts of the world, and to give them a memorable vacation while drawing money into the local economy.

The novelist Julian Barnes exploits this nicely in his novel *England, England.* He imagines the Isle of Wight – a small island just off the southern coast of England – being turned into a miniature version of the whole country, with all the familiar landmarks rebuilt there, and all the familiar events staged there. The busy tourist wouldn't have to bother going even to London, let alone to other well-known sites around the country. Everything would be there.

In the middle of it, Barnes imagines that a role would be found for the monarchy – which is, after all, what many tourists travel to England to see. There would be a king and queen, paid to live in a replica of one of the royal palaces. They would come out onto a balcony at regular times and wave to the crowds. 'Royal' events would be staged so that the tourists would feel they had seen something like the real thing. But of course it would all be a sham. Everybody would know that it was just a huge theme park.

The motive for doing it all, of course, would be money. The motive for the faked 'royal' events in this section of Matthew is more complex.

The soldiers mocking Jesus had nothing to gain financially by dressing him up as a king and pretending to salute him and kneel down before him. They had other things in mind. They had been fighting what today we would call terrorists – Jewish rebels against Rome, desperate for liberty, ready to do anything. The Roman soldiers had probably seen some of their friends killed. They were tired of policing such a place, far away from their homes, having to keep the lid on a volatile and dangerous situation with all kinds of rebel groups ready to riot.

Now here was someone who'd been accused of trying to make himself 'King of the Jews'. He was going to die within hours. Why not have a bit of fun at his expense? Why not tease him, beat him up a bit, show him what the Romans think of other people's 'kings'? Like the 'king' in Julian Barnes' scaled-down England, let's let him know that someone else is in fact boss.

It's hard, reading this story, to remember that this is the same Jesus who, days before, was confronting the authorities in the **Temple**, and who, weeks before, was healing people, celebrating with people, and teaching them about God's **kingdom**. But Matthew has woven hints of all that into the story, to remind us of how Jesus' crucifixion was not a messy accident at the end of a glittering career, but was in fact the proper, though shocking, climax to it.

It isn't just that Jesus is 'enthroned', as it were, on the cross, with the title Matthew wants us to see as the true one written above his head. That, to be sure, is striking in itself. Condemned prisoners regularly had a placard above them, indicating their crime. What for Pilate and the soldiers was Jesus' 'crime' – his claim to be Israel's true king – was for Matthew the sober truth. And the crucifixion was the means by which his kingdom would be established. As he had said to James and John (20.23), there would come a time when he would indeed be enthroned with one person on his right and another on his left; but the throne he had in mind was the cross.

Why? Because the kingdom Jesus had spoken of, from the Sermon on the Mount onwards, was never a kingdom to be established and maintained by military force. If it was to be God's kingdom, it would come about by God's means; and the means that the true God chooses to use are the means of self-giving love. Notice how, in this passage, parts of the Sermon on the Mount come back into play. Jesus himself, at last, is struck about the face by the soldiers, and doesn't retaliate (Matthew 5.39). They take off his outer and inner garments, leaving him naked (Matthew 5.40). As he is going out to be crucified, the soldiers use their 'right' under Roman law to compel someone to carry a burden for them, just as in Matthew 5.41; only this time the burden in question is the heavy crossbeam on which Jesus will be hung.

The point of it all is this: Jesus is leading the way he had spoken of from the beginning, the way of being God's true Israel, the light of the world. He himself is set on a hill, unable now to remain hidden (5.14). This is how he is shining the light of God's love into the dark corners of the world: by taking the evil of the world, the hatred and cruelty and unthinking mockery of the world, the gratuitous violence, bullying and torture that still defaces the world, and letting it do its worst to him. Never let it be said that the Christian **faith** is an airy-fairy thing, all about having wonderful inner, spiritual experiences, and not about the real world. This story takes us to the very heart of what Christianity is all about; and here we meet, close up and raw, the anger and bitterness of the world, doing its worst against one who embodies and represents the love of the creator God himself.

There are three responses, I think, which may be appropriate as we stand and watch this shocking, tragic and yet deeply healing event.

First, we are ourselves of course outraged that such things should happen. Yes, Jesus will say to us, and they are still happening around the world today; what are we doing about it?

Second, we are of course horrified that such things should happen to Jesus himself, this Jesus who had done so many wonderful things, through whom healing and restoration, forgiveness and love came so freely to so many. Yes, Jesus will say to us, and this enthronement now will bring healing, forgiveness and hope to millions more. Do we know it ourselves, and if so are we helping others to know it too?

Third, we are of course overwhelmed, as we realize the full meaning Matthew is putting into the story, at the thought that all this was done *for us*. Yes; and we must learn to be truly grateful, to worship and adore this Jesus in whose death we see the face of God turned towards us in love. As we do so, we too are summoned to follow him, as Matthew is always reminding us, on the same path, the way he described so vividly in the Sermon on the Mount, the way he has now gone himself.

MATTHEW 27.39–44

Jesus Mocked on the Cross

³⁹The people who were going by shouted blasphemies at Jesus. They shook their heads at him.

⁴⁰'So!' they said. 'You were going to destroy the Temple and build it in three days, were you? Save yourself, if you're God's son! Come down from the cross!'

⁴¹The chief priests, too, and the scribes and the elders, mocked him.

⁴²'He rescued others,' they said, 'but he can't rescue himself! All right, so he's the King of Israel! – well, let him come down from the cross right now, and then we'll really believe that he is! ⁴³He trusted in God; let God deliver him now, if he's that keen on him – after all, he did say he was God's son!'

⁴⁴The brigands who were crucified alongside him heaped insults on him as well.

A friend of mine was leading a party of explorers through underground caverns and tunnels. They had trained for this expedition and knew the way. Not all the caves had been explored before, and my friend was convinced that there was a way right through, bringing them out by a different route after some miles underground. It would involve them at one point going down under water inside the cave, in order to come up the other side in a continuing tunnel. Nobody had even attempted to go this way before.

But when they got to the crucial point in the cave, some of the party lost their nerve. It was a stupid idea, they said. There were no maps, no charts to indicate that there was a way through. They might go down into the water and simply drown while trying to find the way forward. Some got angry with the leader. What right had he got, they said, to push them into doing something crazy just because he had the dream of finding a new way? Eventually he realized there was only one thing to do. He would have to go through himself and find the way, and then come back to take them with him.

As he went down into the water, some of the group stood there nervously silent, but the ones who had objected laughed at him. So much for your great dreams, they said. Either you'll come back soaked and defeated or you won't come back at all. That's what happens to people who think they know too much and discover too late that they don't.

Of course – I wouldn't be telling the story otherwise! – he did find the way through, and eventually they all followed, including the grumblers. But the point of the story, as you will see, is to show what it was like as Jesus pioneered the way through death and out the other side into the new life that he knew was there but which nobody else understood.

In the previous passage, the pagan soldiers were mocking Jesus because he'd been called the King of the Jews – the charge he was accused of before Pilate. In this passage, though, we are back with the Jewish leaders, the chief **priests** and the rest. They are throwing back in Jesus' face the claims he had made, directly and indirectly, about the **Temple**, about himself, and particularly about the question of his being the unique **son of God**, the true **Messiah**.

With this, Matthew takes us back to the story of Jesus' hearing before Caiaphas, where all this came together (26.59–66). He reminds us of all the times in the previous chapters where Jesus has said and done things which meant that the Temple would be destroyed. But there is more. As in the previous section we found our minds going back all the way to the Sermon on the Mount, so here Matthew leads us to an even earlier part of his story: Jesus' **baptism** and temptation.

It was in Jesus' baptism that God told him, clearly and dramatically: you are my son, I am delighted with you (3.17). Jesus had lived all his public career in the belief that God had indeed spoken those words, confirming the vocation of which he had been aware, we may suppose, from much earlier. Now this belief was to face the sternest and roughest challenge.

It was in his temptation, of course, that the challenge had begun. As we look back at the story (4.1–11), we see how it points directly to the mocking of the Jewish leaders. If you really are God's son, said the tempter, surely it's wrong that you should be hungry like this? If you really are God's son, why don't you show people the dramatic ways in which God will look after you? If you really are God's son, why don't you take the quick way and come to your **kingdom** in one easy move? Now, in almost exactly the same tone of voice, we find the mockers challenging him: If you really are God's son, why don't you do what you said – destroy the Temple and rebuild it? If you really are God's son, why don't you come down from the cross? If you really are God's son, why doesn't God deliver you? Surely he can't want you to be hanging there in agony? Surely he doesn't want you to ... *die*?

Jesus answered the temptations in chapter 4 with quotations from scripture. This time he remains silent; but inwardly, we may suppose, his deep well of biblical learning and devotion had not run dry. When, in the next section (verse 46), he cries out the opening words of Psalm 22, it is as though that is his answer to the mockery, even though the answer comes this time in the form of a complaint to God himself. But Matthew intends us to understand that here too, on the cross, we are to learn something about the whole ministry which Jesus has had, which is reaching its grand finale in his crucifixion.

Between the temptations of chapter 4 and the mocking on the cross stands Jesus' entire public career. During that time, as we have seen, he was challenged and confronted many times by the leaders, actual or self-appointed, of his own Jewish people and their public opinion. They accused him of breaking the **law**. They accused him of being in league with the devil. They refused to believe that the way he was going was the true way to God's kingdom. They were like the explorers confronting their leader as he was inviting them to trust him and follow him through the deep and dark water to the new tunnel he believed was the other side. They weren't having it. It was madness. They knew how God's kingdom ought to come. Jesus' alternative way held no attraction for them, even though he backed up his invitation with so many remarkable deeds of power.

Now, Matthew is explaining, we see where it was all leading. Opposition and rejection from his own people combined with the hatred and anger of the non-Jewish world to put Jesus on the cross, and this was in fact the hidden secret of his whole public career. Jesus didn't, as it were, have an early period of success followed by a later period of failure and defeat. Of course, many were excited by his dramatic work and teaching, but even they were following him with a different end in view. Some will have been thrilled by his vision of the present Temple being destroyed to make way for something new that God would do; the present Temple was, after all, being run by the chief priests, for their own benefit, in a way that many found repellent and oppressive. But nobody had ever imagined it would end like this.

Nobody, that is, except Jesus himself. From his baptism onwards he had known what lay ahead: a path that went down into the deep water, like Israel going into the Red Sea. He had trusted, not that God would deliver him by taking him back again to the dry land from which he'd come, but that God would take him through the water and up the other side, leading him on to the promised land that lay ahead. This was the true-Israel path, the **Exodus** path, the path that led through death itself to a new world, a new life, the other side. He wasn't simply going to defeat the Romans, or for that matter the chief priests. He was going to defeat death itself. But to do that he had to lead the way through; and in that he had to endure the mockery of those who said he was mad, deluded, just another fanatic who imagines he's God's chosen one only to find out too late that he's mistaken. If he really was God's son, surely he would come down from the cross?

But, as Matthew expects us to know, it is *because* he is God's son that he must stay on the cross. That is the way the world will be saved. That is how death will be defeated. That is how he will finish the work the father has given him to do. That is how the father's delight will be complete.

And, as we watch in awe and gratitude, we hear the voice that says to us: you, too, are my beloved child. Are you ready to follow me, whatever people will say?

MATTHEW 27.45–56

The Death of God's Son

[45]From noon until mid-afternoon there was darkness over the whole land. [46]About the middle of the afternoon Jesus shouted out in a loud voice,

'Eli, Eli, lema sabachthani!'

– which means, 'My God, my God, what did you abandon me for?'

⁴⁷Some of the people who were standing there heard it and said, 'This fellow's calling Elijah!'

⁴⁸One of them ran at once and got a sponge. He filled it with vinegar, put it on a reed, and gave him a drink.

⁴⁹The others said, 'Wait a bit. Let's see if Elijah is going to come and rescue him!'

⁵⁰But Jesus shouted out loudly one more time, and then breathed his last breath.

⁵¹At that instant the Temple curtain was torn in two, from top to bottom. The earth shook, the rocks were split, ⁵²and the tombs burst open. Many bodies of the sleeping holy ones were raised. ⁵³They came out of the tombs after Jesus' resurrection, and went into the holy city, where they appeared to several people.

⁵⁴When the centurion and the others with him, keeping watch over Jesus, saw the earthquake and the things that happened, they were scared out of their wits.

'He really was God's son!' they said.

In many Christian bookshops around the world today you can buy posters to hang on the wall which remind you of some aspect of the Christian faith and life. Often they have biblical texts, set against a background of glorious scenery. Sometimes they are funny. Sometimes they include poems, or short meditations.

One of the best known of these is called 'Footprints'. It tells of someone looking back over their life, lived in trust with God, seeing it like a set of footprints through the sand. There are two sets of footprints most of the way; you and God, as it were, walking side by side. But sometimes – and they were always the hardest times – there was only one set. Why, you ask, did God abandon you at that moment? Back comes the answer: in those times, my child, I was carrying you.

It is important to say, right at the start of this section, that this is not a helpful way of understanding this story. When

Jesus cried out, in the opening words of Psalm 22, asking why God had abandoned him, Matthew does not intend us to think, in a comforting sort of way, 'Oh, that was all right; you see, it only *felt* like that. Actually, God was carrying him through.' Part of the whole point of the cross is that there the weight of the world's evil really did converge upon Jesus, blotting out the sunlight of God's love as surely as the light of day was blotted out for three hours. (Matthew probably intends us to see here the start of the fulfilment of Jesus' words in 24.29; these events are ushering in God's 'last days', which will reach their climax when the **son of man** is exalted and vindicated, and the **Temple** is destroyed.) Jesus is 'giving his life as a ransom for many' (20.28), and the sin of the 'many', which he is bearing, has for the first and only time in his experience caused a cloud to come between him and the father he loved and obeyed, the one who had been delighted in him.

Of course, Psalm 22 goes on, after a long catalogue of suffering, to speak of God's vindication of the sufferer, and of the establishment of God's **kingdom** (Psalm 22.22–31). But that isn't what Matthew wants us to think of here. He simply notes the reaction of those standing by, who mishear what Jesus said, and imagined from the repeated word 'Eli!' that Jesus was shouting to Elijah, calling for the great prophet to come and rescue him.

That, we may suppose, was the last thing on Jesus' mind, though it fitted with some of the speculations of the time. Matthew, however, wants us to think back to the other times when Elijah has appeared, or been spoken of, in this **gospel**, notably in the transfiguration (17.1–9) and in Jesus' sayings about **John the Baptist** (17.10–13). Elijah has already come, not to rescue Jesus from this fate but precisely to point him towards it, assuring him that he is going the way God has commanded.

Finally he arrives at the goal. Jesus' death – described by

Matthew as 'breathing his last' or 'giving up his **spirit**' – is the point towards which the gospel has been moving all along. He has remained obedient to the end, even through the period of God-forsakenness that formed the heart, strangely, of his God-given mission. He takes with him, into the darkness of death, the sin of the world: my sin, your sin, the sin of countless millions, the weight that has hung around the world's neck and dragged it down to destruction.

And the world itself – the physical, natural world – is the first to respond. As one recent writer has put it, the end of Jesus is the end of the world in miniature. In particular, it is the end of the Temple in miniature: the beautiful curtain that hung across the entrance to the inner sanctuary is torn in two, presumably by the force of the earthquake that shook the city. Judgment has been hanging over the Temple for several chapters now in Matthew; the **priests** have themselves finally rejected Jesus (verses 41–43); now their power base, the centre of their world, receives a symbolic destruction as potent as the action of Jesus himself a few days earlier (20.12–14). Jesus' death is the beginning of the end for the system that had opposed him, that had refused to heed his summons, that had denied its vocation to be the light of the world, the city set on a hill to which the nations would flock.

Instead, the nations will now flock to a different hill: to the hill called Calvary, outside the city walls, where the king of the Jews has died a cruel and shameful death. As a sign of what is to come (and looking back to the wise men of 2.1–12, the centurion of 8.5–13, and the Canaanite woman of 15.21–28), we see another centurion, standing guard at the foot of the cross, giving voice to the confession of **faith** that millions more would make, in shocked surprise at the sudden revelation of God's truth where one would least expect it: 'He really was God's son!'

That is what Matthew intends and expects his readers to say

as they, whether Jewish or **Gentile**, look at the death of Jesus and the earth-shattering things that have resulted. Whatever we think about the earthquake, and the bodies of God's people of old being raised from the dead – and it has to be said that this is one of the oddest tales anywhere in the New Testament – we who live so much later do not have to look to one or two extraordinary occurrences at the time in order to be able to say that Jesus' death has changed the shape of the world.

Look at it like this. The effect of his giving of his own life; the example of love, non-retaliation, the kingdom-way of confronting evil with goodness; Jesus' taking of the world's hatred and anger on to himself; and, way beyond all of these, the defeat of the powers of evil, the blotting out of the sins of the world, the love of God shining through the dark clouds of wickedness – all of this is now to be seen around the world. It is seen, not only in the millions who worship Jesus and thank him for his death, but in the work of healing which flows from it: in reconciliation and hope, for communities and for individuals. The world is indeed a different place because of what Jesus did in his death.

Beyond all this again, Matthew wants us to look on to the final restoration, God's great new world (19.28), the time of renewal. God is already making all things new, and the death of Jesus is the key event through which this can now happen.

But it all begins, to our astonishment, with some of those who had died and been buried long since. It isn't quite clear what Matthew wants us to think here. Did these 'sleeping' bodies wake up at Jesus' death, but wait until Easter morning to go into the city? What did they do then? What happened to them? These and similar questions have encouraged some to think that Matthew intends us to see the story as picture-language, a vivid way of saying 'from that moment on, death was a defeated force'. Or he may simply, in reporting stories told at the time and afterwards, be happy to leave this as a loose end in his own narrative, a way of saying, 'From now on, you never know what God's lifegiving power will achieve!' It was, of course, a hint of what would come at the end of all things, the great final **resurrection** of which Paul and others speak.

Certainly Matthew intends that as we read this story we should look ahead to the full results of Jesus' death. The **disciples**, including the women watching from a distance, see only darkness, gloom and death. But Matthew's reader already knows what they will discover three days later: that this death was not the failure of Jesus to show himself as the **son of God**, but the way in which his identity, vocation and mission were confirmed and accomplished. As we join our voices with the centurion and others, in declaring that Jesus was indeed God's son, so we commit ourselves to living by that faith, and to learning every day, by looking at the son, more about the love of the father.

MATTHEW 27.57–66

The Burial of Jesus

[57]When evening came, a rich man from Arimathea arrived. He was called Joseph, and he, too, was a disciple of Jesus. [58]He went to Pilate and requested the body of Jesus. Pilate gave the order that it should be given to him.

[59]So Joseph took the body and wrapped it in a clean linen cloth. [60]He laid it in his own new tomb, which he had carved out of the rock. Then he rolled a large stone across the doorway of the tomb, and went away.

[61]Mary Magdalene was there, and so was the other Mary. They were sitting opposite the tomb.

[62]On the next day (that is, the day after Preparation Day), the chief priests and the Pharisees went as a group to Pilate.

[63]'Sir,' they said, 'when that deceiver was still alive, we recall that he said, "After three days, I'll rise again." [64]So please give

the order for the tomb to be made secure until the third day. Otherwise his disciples might come and steal him away, and then tell the people, "He's been raised from the dead!", and so the last deception would be worse than the first.'

⁶⁵'You may have a guard,' said Pilate; 'make it as secure as you know how.' ⁶⁶So they went and made the tomb secure, sealing the stone and putting a guard on watch.

I was never much good at chess, but I have from time to time played against some reasonably good players and I remember what it felt like. There was always a point, usually quite early on, when I simply wouldn't understand what they were doing. They would move a rook here, a knight there, move the queen somewhere else, and all without apparent connection or plan. Then, a few moves later, when I thought I was about to do something really clever, one of the pieces that had innocently been moved earlier on was there, blocking my way. The mark of a good player is to anticipate the moves the opponent is going to make, and to block them before they can happen.

That is more or less exactly what Matthew is doing in describing Jesus' burial. Of course there is more to it than that: there is devotion, sorrow, awe; there is gratitude to Joseph of Arimathea for being in the right place at the right time. But in many ways the burial story is actually an anticipation of the **resurrection** story. Matthew is moving the necessary chess pieces into place for the game he knows will take place.

The central claim of the early church was, of course, that Jesus of Nazareth had been raised from the dead. The central claim wasn't that he was a great teacher, a powerful healer, an inspiring leader, or that he was the victim of a gross miscarriage of justice. All of those were true, but they wouldn't add up to the early Christian **faith** and life. The crucial fact, they believed, was that Jesus had been bodily raised to life after being well and truly dead and buried. This is what they announced to the startled world, the world of Jews and **Gentiles**.

And of course people laughed at them, and offered alternative explanations. He wasn't really dead, they said. Or maybe the **disciples** stole the body. Or maybe someone else did. Or perhaps the women went to the wrong tomb. These were all stock answers to the early Christian **message**, and we may suppose that from early on stock responses were developed – which then, like the skilful chess moves, could be made in advance, before the main story was even told, to rule out the wrong answers beforehand.

So the first point is that the tomb was new, readily recognizable, and sealed with a large stone. We need to pause here for a moment, because in most cultures today people don't bury the dead in the way they did in Jesus' day. Most Jews in Palestine at that time were buried in caves, sometimes underneath the houses where they had lived. The bodies weren't put in coffins, or burnt to ashes, but wrapped in a cloth along with perfumes and spices. The body would then be put on a shelf or ledge inside the cave. Then, when the flesh had all decomposed, friends or relatives would collect the bones, fold them up neatly, and put them in a bone-box (known as an 'ossuary'). Often several bodies would be on ledges in the same tomb. In this case, as Matthew has carefully explained, the tomb was new, and there were no other bodies in it.

Grave-robbery was common in the ancient world, so many cave-tombs had huge circular stones, sometimes measuring as much as two metres in diameter, which people would roll across the mouth of the cave to prevent anyone getting in without a great struggle. This is what Joseph did. You can still see some tombs of this sort in the Middle East.

The fact that Joseph requested Jesus' body from Pilate, and that Pilate granted the request, shows well enough that Jesus was indeed dead. Roman soldiers and governors didn't go in for half-measures when it came to carrying out capital sentences. Any possibility that they had let a condemned rebel leader escape death can be left out of the question. Likewise, the fact that Jesus' main disciples had nothing to do with the whole procedure, but were in hiding, indicates well enough that they wouldn't have been in a position to steal the body. Nor, indeed, could anyone else; the chief **priests**, anxious to avoid such a thing, obtained a guard of Roman soldiers from Pilate. They themselves sealed the stone to make sure it wasn't moved.

There remains the question of the identification of the tomb. Matthew is careful to note that the two women who went to the tomb on Easter morning (28.1) were there on the Friday evening (27.61), and saw exactly where it was.

None of this, of course, proves that the Christian story is true. Nor does the next chapter. From the very beginning there has been room for doubt, and many have taken that option. But Matthew is concerned that the doubt be located in the right place. There was no confusion about the details of the burial. If you are going to doubt whether Jesus was raised from the dead it must be because you doubt whether the living God could or would do such a thing for Israel's **Messiah**, the one on whose shoulders rested the weight of the world's salvation. That is what is at stake.

As we watch the burial of Jesus, and meditate on his going before us into the tomb which is the common lot of humanity, we stand in awe once more at the thought that he, alone of all the human race, has found the way through it and out into God's new world beyond. Matthew can hardly wait, we may imagine, to take the story into the next chapter where all is revealed.

MATTHEW 28.1–10

The Resurrection of Jesus

| [1]Dawn was breaking on the first day of the week; the sabbath |

was over. Mary Magdalene, and the other Mary, had come to look at the tomb, [2]when suddenly there was a great earthquake. An angel of the Lord came down from heaven. He came to the stone, rolled it away, and sat down on top of it. [3]Looking at him was like looking at lightning, and his clothes were white, like snow. [4]The guards trembled with terror at him, and became like corpses themselves.

[5]'Don't be afraid,' said the angel to the women. 'I know you're looking for Jesus, who was crucified. [6]He isn't here! He's been raised, as he said he would be! Come and see the place where he was lying – [7]and then go at once, and tell his disciples that he's been raised from the dead, and that he's going on ahead of you to Galilee. That's where you'll see him. There: I've told you.'

[8]The women scurried off quickly, away from the tomb, in a mixture of terror and great delight, and went to tell his disciples. [9]Suddenly, there was Jesus himself. He met them and said, 'Greetings!' They came up to him and took hold of his feet, prostrating themselves in front of him.

[10]'Don't be afraid,' said Jesus to them. 'Go and tell my brothers that I'm going off to Galilee. Tell them they'll see me there.'

Everyone above a certain age, in the Western world at least, can remember where they were when they heard that President Kennedy had been assassinated. Many people in other parts of the world will be able to remember where they were and what they were doing at similar moments of great national and international crisis.

Many of us also remember clearly the precise moment when something startling and very, very good happened to us. I have a vivid memory, nearly thirty years ago as I write this, of the telephone call which told me that I had been appointed to my first job, a position I had set my heart on. I remember being, for once in my life, completely lost for words; the person who had called me had to repeat what he'd said before I could eventually stammer out my thanks. I remember the dry sense in my throat as I put the telephone down and called to my wife to tell her the news. I knew that from that moment on my life was going to be different. A whole new world was opening up in front of me.

It isn't difficult to understand the mixture of terror and delight that gripped the women who had gone to the tomb that morning. Mark and Luke explain that they had brought spices, since the burial had taken place in too much of a hurry (before the start of the **sabbath** on Friday evening) to wrap the body in the proper way. Matthew simply says that they had come to look at the tomb. At that point in the story they seem simply to be mourners, just wanting to be there, near Jesus, to pour out their sorrow in as much peace and quiet as possible.

Peace and quiet was the last thing they got. Matthew's grave-side scene is easily the most dramatic of the four: an earthquake, an angel, the guards stunned into a swoon, and messages about Jesus going on ahead to Galilee. Some think, of course, that Matthew has added some of these details to make things appear more spectacular; you might just as well say, though, that the others missed them out because, if you're telling a story like this around the world, you don't want people to laugh at the details and then think they've dismissed the event itself. For Matthew, standing within a long Jewish tradition in which angels tended to appear at great moments within God's purposes, this wasn't a problem.

The point, of course, is that what is happening is the action of God himself. The God who remained apparently silent on Good Friday is having the last word. He is answering the unspoken questions of Jesus' followers, and the spoken question of Jesus himself on the cross. And what God is doing is not just an extraordinary **miracle**, a display of supernatural power for its own sake, or a special favour to Jesus. What God is doing is starting something new, beginning the new world promised long ago, sending the **disciples** to Galilee in the first place but then, as we shall see, on to the ends of the earth and the close of the age with the news of what has happened. A whole new world was opening up in front of them.

Though they were thunderstruck with amazement and fear, there is every reason to suppose that they remembered for the rest of their lives what had happened that day. The accounts of those first few moments go back to genuine personal memory, told again and again to incredulous friends and neighbours, in the tone of voice of someone saying 'I know – I almost couldn't believe it myself! It still seems totally amazing. But this is how it was.'

Though the angel tells the women that the disciples are to go to Galilee and see Jesus there, they meet him almost at once, there near the tomb. Luke simply records appearances of Jesus in the Jerusalem area; Matthew and John record them both in Jerusalem and in Galilee. (Mark's final chapter is almost certainly broken off; in the eight verses which are left, he simply has the angels instructing the women, as here, to tell the disciples to go to Galilee to see Jesus there.) But the crucial thing is that Jesus' **resurrection** is not about proving some point, or offering people a new spiritual experience. It is about God's purpose that must now be fulfilled. They must see Jesus, but that seeing will be a commissioning, a commissioning to a new work, a new life, a new way of life in which everything he told them before will start to come true.

We cannot today meet Jesus in the way the women did that morning. Of course, it is a vital part of Christian belief and experience that we can and should meet Jesus in **spirit**, and get to know him as we worship him and learn from him. That personal and intimate relationship with the living Lord is central to what being a Christian means in practice. But we would be seriously misreading Matthew, not to mention the other **gospel** writers, if we thought his story was just a vivid or coded way for describing that experience. He clearly intended to write of something that had actually happened, something that had not only changed the women's hearts but had torn a hole in normal history. This event had changed the world for ever. It announced, not as a theory but as a fact, that God's **kingdom** had come, that the **son of man** had been vindicated after his suffering, and that there was dawning not just another day, another week in the history of Israel and the world, but the start of God's new age that would continue until the nations had been brought into obedience.

Take away the resurrection of Jesus, in fact, and you leave Matthew without a gospel. The cross is the climax of his story, but it only makes the sense it does as the cross of the one who was then raised from the dead. The great discourses of the gospel – the Sermon on the Mount, and all the rest – are his way of saying that Jesus is the new Moses, but much more than that, Israel's **Messiah**. He is the one who is giving Israel and the world the new **Law** through which God's new way of being human has been unveiled before the world. But all this is true only because the one who proclaimed God's blessings on his followers, the one who announced God's woes on those who went their own ways, and the one who spoke God's kingdom-message in **parables**, is now the risen Lord.

Think back through the whole gospel. Watch how one part after another springs to new life as the one of whom Matthew speaks is now revealed as the one through whom death itself is defeated.

MATTHEW 28.11–15

The Priests and the Guards

[11]While the women were on their way, some of the soldiers who had been on guard went into the city and told the chief priests everything that had happened. [12]They called an emergency meeting with the elders, allotted a substantial sum of money, and gave it to the soldiers.

> [13]'This', they told them, 'is what you are to say: "His disciples came in the night, while we were asleep, and stole him away." [14]And if this gets reported to the governor, we'll explain it to him and make sure you stay out of trouble.'
>
> [15]They took the money and did as they had been instructed. And this story still goes the rounds among the Jews to this day.

In the world of science, there is a particular form of behaviour that occurs when a long-held belief is under attack.

The most famous instance of it was when Copernicus (1473–1543) argued that Earth and the other planets go round the sun, instead of the sun and everything else going round Earth as everyone had thought up until then. This was utterly revolutionary, and it took another century of research, from people like Kepler, Galileo and Newton, before Copernicus's ideas became universally accepted by scientists.

Before that happened, there were many people, anxious to protect their current world-view, who did their best to argue against the new theory. Copernicus had observed many new things about the behaviour of the sun and the planets; very well, they would seek to explain these new things within the old system. Anything rather than admit that the system itself was faulty and needed a radical overhaul.

Something similar went on in the first century, and continues to go on today, when people are faced with the story of Jesus' **resurrection**. In this passage Matthew returns to the chess-game once more, to ward off more thoroughly a move that was regularly made in his day to enable people to avoid coming to terms with the resurrection as an actual event. He knows the line of attack that is regularly employed among the non-Christian Jews of his day: the **disciples**, they say, came at night and stole his body. Ah, says Matthew, that's what the chief **priests** paid the guards to say. You're simply repeating a frantic and unlikely tale that people told when they'd been well bribed to do so.

Of course, someone might say, Matthew would say that, wouldn't he? Yes, but think what he had to gain and lose by it. Denying the resurrection left everybody's world-view intact. The Jews could continue as they had done. The Romans could go on running the world their way. Philosophers could still debate their lofty doctrines. Nobody would need to make radical readjustments. But if the resurrection of Jesus was true, and if people were to start reordering their lives by it, they would be on a collision course with the rest of the world. Matthew knew that as well as we do.

In fact, what the Jewish leaders did in this story is not very different from what generations of sceptics have done ever since. Don't be fooled by the idea that modern science has disproved the resurrection of Jesus. Modern science has done no such thing. Everybody in the ancient world, just like everybody in the modern world, knew perfectly well that dead people don't get resurrected. It didn't take Copernicus or Newton, or Einstein for that matter, to prove that; just universal observation of universal facts. The Christian belief is not that some people sometimes get raised from the dead, and Jesus happens to be one of them. It is precisely that people don't ever get raised from the dead, and that something new has happened in and through Jesus which has blown a hole through previous observations. The Christian thus agrees with scientists ancient and modern: yes, dead people don't rise. But the Christian goes on to say that something new and different has now occurred in the case of Jesus. This isn't because there was an odd glitch in the cosmos, or something peculiar about Jesus' biochemistry, but because the God who made the world, and who called Israel to be the bearer of his rescue-operation for the world, was at work in and through Jesus to remake the world. The resurrection was the dramatic launching of this project.

From the beginning, therefore, Christianity is committed to

explaining itself and arguing its case before the watching world. Ironically, the world has often accused Christianity of hanging on to its belief in Jesus' resurrection in the face of supposed scientific evidence that shows it was impossible. In fact, since the impossibility of resurrection has always been well known, it begins to look as though things are the other way around. Not only first-century Jews, with their particular agendas that they didn't want disturbed, but people of every age, find the resurrection of Jesus threatening. It isn't a matter of finding new evidence on the matter; there isn't any. The resurrection is like Copernicus's startling new discoveries that were destined to change for ever the way we look at the world.

People often flail around in desperation to find an alternative explanation for the empty tomb, for the appearances of Jesus, for the rise of the early church which had Jesus' resurrection as its central belief. They come up with all sorts of unlikely suggestions, just as Copernicus's opponents came up with all sorts of ideas which tried to get his new evidence within the framework of their old, comfortable world-view. It doesn't work. Resurrection is here to stay.

In particular, the movement in Western culture known as the Enlightenment, which swept through philosophy and politics in the eighteenth century, producing the French Revolution, the American Constitution, and many other phenomena, always tried to make out that it had done away with previous superstitions and was replacing them with rational, 'enlightened', views. These, it claimed, would free people from intellectual and political tyranny. In fact, the opposite is the case. Granted, the movement brought great blessings, such as modern medicine and communications. It also brought great curses – not only the French Revolution itself, which killed thousands of its own people in the name of liberty and equality for all, but also the terrifying totalitarianisms of the twentieth century. The selfishness which keeps the West economically prosperous while much of the rest of the world remains poor is itself part of 'Enlightenment' philosophy.

No wonder, then, such a world-view wants to resist the news of Jesus' resurrection every bit as much as the chief priests did. No wonder it bribes people in all kinds of subtle ways to tell stories in which Jesus didn't really rise from the dead. No wonder it tries to make out that Christianity is just the invention of a few cunning individuals trying to feather their own nests. (This always was an absurd charge, of course; it was three centuries before anyone gained anything except insults, danger, torture and death by believing in the resurrection.) All the while, of course, by denying the resurrection, the 'modern' world-view, and many other ones too, want to preserve their own status quo intact against the radical disruption that would otherwise occur.

What the chief priests arranged with the guards was not, in fact, a purely first-century phenomenon. Matthew has alerted us to a recurring feature of Christian **faith**: the need to argue for the the truth of Easter, and to expose and demolish rival attempts to say what happened. Those who believe in the resurrection need to be constantly on the alert against attack. They also need, of course, to be sure that they are themselves allowing the resurrection to blow constantly like a fresh breeze through their own lives, thoughts and imaginations. There's no point defending and explaining God's new world if you're still living in the old one yourself.

MATTHEW 28.16–20

The Great Commission

[16]So the eleven disciples went off to Galilee, to the mountain where Jesus had instructed them to go. [17]There they saw him, and worshipped him, though some hesitated.

[18]Jesus came towards them and addressed them.

'All authority in heaven and on earth', he said, 'has been given to me! [19]So you must go and make all the nations into disciples. Baptize them in the name of the father, and of the son, and of the holy spirit. [20]Teach them to observe everything I have commanded you. And look: I am with you, every single day, to the very end of the age.'

You sometimes wonder, when listening to some of the great classical composers, whether they really know how to bring a piece to an end.

One of the most notorious is Beethoven. There are times when, at the end of a symphony, you think you're just coming to the end, but the chords go crashing on and on, sounding almost 'final' but leaving room for just one more . . . and then another . . . and then another . . . until the very last one dies away and the symphony is truly complete. No doubt a serious student of music would explain that there was a purpose in it, but for many listeners it seems as though a great deal has been packed into the ending, almost as though the whole symphony is being gathered up into those last few explosive chords.

Matthew's ending is much like that. Not that it goes on longer than we expect; it is in fact quite compact. But it contains so much that we would do well to slow down in our reading of these final verses and ponder each line, indeed each phrase, to see how they gather up the whole **gospel** and pack it tight into the final meeting between Jesus and his followers.

The scene begins on a mountain. No surprises there: a great deal in Matthew happens on a mountain. The temptations; the Sermon on the Mount; the transfiguration; the final discourse on the Mount of Olives; and now this parting scene. Moses and Elijah met the living God on a mountain, and they have appeared in this gospel talking with Jesus; now Jesus invites his **disciples** to meet him, so that they can be commissioned in turn.

What does surprise us is that, according to Matthew, some of them hesitated. The word can actually mean 'doubt', though we can't be sure how much of that Matthew means here. Did they hesitate over, or doubt, whether it was truly Jesus? Or did they hesitate over, or doubt, whether they, as good Jewish monotheists, believing in YHWH as the one true God, should actually *worship* Jesus? It isn't clear.

What is clear is that the majority of them did worship Jesus, and that Matthew firmly believes this was the right reaction. On several previous occasions in the gospel he has used this word ('worship') to describe people coming reverently to Jesus. Usually it seems to mean simply that they prostrated themselves before him, adopting an attitude of reverence though not necessarily implying that they thought he was divine. (See 8.2; 9.18; 14.33; 15.25; 20.20; and indeed 28.9.) Now, however, to jump for a moment to the last line of the book, it is clear that Matthew wants us to see that in Jesus the promise of the very first chapter has been fulfilled. Jesus is the 'Emmanuel', the one in whom 'God is with us' (1.23). Now he declares that he himself is 'with you always'. The only appropriate reaction to this is indeed worship, worship of the one true God who is now, astonishingly, revealed in and as Jesus himself.

In particular, Jesus has now been given 'all authority in **heaven** and earth'. We recall that in the temptations the devil offered Jesus this prestige, but without exacting the price that he has now paid (4.8–10). That would have been a hollow triumph, leading to the worst tyranny imaginable. Jesus' authority as the risen one, by contrast, is the authority of the one who has defeated tyranny itself, the ultimate tyranny of death; his is the authority under which life, God's new life, can begin to flourish. Despite what many people today suppose, it is basic to the most elementary New Testament **faith** that Jesus is *already* ruling the whole world. That is one of the most important results of his **resurrection**; it is part of the meaning of **messiahship**, which his new life after the crucifixion has made plain.

People get very puzzled by the claim that Jesus is already ruling the world, until they see what is in fact being said. The claim is not that the world is already completely as Jesus intends it to be. The claim is that he is working to take it from where it was – under the rule not only of death but of corruption, greed and every kind of wickedness – and to bring it, by slow means and quick, under the rule of his life-giving love. And how is he doing this? Here is the shock: *through us, his followers*. The project only goes forward insofar as Jesus' agents, the people he has commissioned, are taking it forward.

Many today mock this claim just as much as they mock the resurrection itself. The church in its various forms has got so much wrong, has made so many mistakes, has let its Lord down so often, that many people, including many who love Jesus for themselves, despair of it and suppose that nothing will ever change until Jesus himself returns to sort it all out. But that isn't Matthew's belief, and it doesn't fit with what we know of Jesus' commissioning of his followers in Luke, Acts and John. It doesn't fit with Paul's vision of his task. They all agree with Matthew: those who believe in Jesus, who are witnesses to his resurrection, are given the responsibility to go and make real in the world the authority which he already has. This, after all, is part of the answer to the prayer that God's **kingdom** will come on earth as in heaven. If we pray that prayer, we shouldn't be surprised if we are called upon to help bring about God's answer to it.

The tasks Jesus leaves his followers, tasks which will bring his sovereign authority to bear on the world, are straightforward enough to outline, though daunting and demanding to put into practice. The first is to *make disciples.* As Jesus called the fishermen by the sea of Galilee, and trained them up as 'learners', imitating his way of life and coming little by little to understand his kingdom-message, so his followers ever since have the responsibility of calling men, women and children to follow him, and training them to understand and follow his message and his way. Evangelism – announcing God's **good news**, focused on Jesus, to bring people to faith and obedience – remains central to the way in which Jesus' authority is brought to bear on the world.

The second task is to *baptize* them. **Baptism** is not an optional extra for followers of Jesus. Jesus himself linked baptism to his own death; part of the meaning of baptism is to commit us, through plunging into water, to dying with Jesus and coming to share his new life. (Paul spells this out in Romans 6, but many other passages imply it, including the present one.) Baptism is the public, physical and visible way in which someone is marked out, branded almost, with the holy 'name'. As Jesus was given, by the angel, the name 'Jesus', signifying his real identity and the task that lay before him, so now, with his work complete, we suddenly discover that the 'name' which we are all to share is the new 'name' of the living God – the father, the son and the **holy spirit**.

Matthew innocently places this formula on Jesus' lips, unaware that in centuries to come it would become well-known as a brilliant piece of dogmatic theology. He is, at this point, rather like someone innocently whistling a snatch of tune that a great composer will later make the centrepiece of a wonderful oratorio. Throughout the gospel he has shown us that Jesus knew himself to be, in a special sense, the unique son of the God he (and Israel as a whole) knew as 'father'. This went with his being specially equipped for his task with the 'holy spirit', the spirit who gave him the power to do what he did, and the status of being God's 'anointed' (e.g. 3.16; 12.28). Now, apparently, those who have followed Jesus and have become true disciples are themselves to be caught up in this divine life and purpose. What happened to and through Jesus in the unique gospel story is to be repeated as the message goes out into the **Gentile** world.

The third thing they must do is to *teach*. The gospel of Jesus generates a lifestyle quite different from the way the world lives. Jesus has already highlighted this at various levels, from the personal morality outlined in the Sermon on the Mount to the high demand for forgiveness in chapter 18, and not least to the overturning of the normal way rulers behave (20.25–27). But doubtless Matthew wants us to think particularly of the five great blocks of Jesus' teaching around which the gospel is constructed. These are to be the basis of what the church must teach the new disciples.

This task remains unfinished in our own day. If Christians around the world gave as much energy to it as they do to learning so many other things, worthy in themselves but none so important as this, we would make more headway with the gospel than we usually seem to do.

But Jesus never leaves people simply with a list of commands to keep. The three instructions he has given are held in place by the promises at the beginning and end of the passage. The reason we are to do these things is because he already possesses all authority; the promise which sustains us in the task is that he is with us always and for ever. He is, as we have said, the Emmanuel. God-with-us turns into Jesus-with-us. There is no greater personal promise than that.

From the height of this final mountain we look out at God's future from Jesus' perspective, and what do we see?

We see, first, the astonishing early results of the gospel. In AD 25 nobody outside a small town in Galilee had heard of Jesus. By AD 50 there were riots in Rome because of him, and by AD 65 his followers were being persecuted by the emperor himself. All roads led to Rome; once Rome knew of something, everywhere else knew quite soon afterwards. Jesus' claim to an authority higher than kings and emperors was made good over and over again in the lives, and often enough the deaths, of his followers.

We see, second, the fall of Jerusalem in AD 70. Jesus had warned of what would happen to the city and **Temple** if it refused his message; the warnings came horribly true. This, as we saw in chapter 24, is part of the meaning of 'the end'. It was, in all sorts of senses, the end of the world for the Israel of old, the end for the chief **priests**, the **Pharisees**, and all who had made the Temple the centre of their way of life.

But out beyond these events we see a greater future. The **'age to come'** has already broken in to the 'present age'. But, as Paul makes so clear, not until death itself is destroyed, and the whole world comes under the rule of Jesus, will God's purpose be fully accomplished. How are we to conceive of this?

To answer, we come back to the Lord's Prayer once more, set by Matthew at the heart of Jesus' great Sermon (6.9–13), and forming a fitting way for us to take our leave of this great gospel. Bread, forgiveness and deliverance are, of course, always going to be needed as long as the present world continues. But there will come a time when those needs are swallowed up in the complete life of the new age: when God's will is done on earth as in heaven, because heaven and earth have been joined together in the new creation; when God's kingdom, established by Jesus in his death and resurrection, has finally conquered all its enemies by the power of the divine love; and when, in line with the ancient hopes of Israel, and now with the central intention of Jesus himself, the name of God is honoured, hallowed, exalted and celebrated throughout the whole creation. Every time we say the words 'Our father...' we are pleading for that day to be soon, and pledging ourselves to work to bring it closer.

GLOSSARY

accuser, *see* **the satan**

age to come, *see* **present age**

apostle, disciple, the Twelve

'Apostle' means 'one who is sent'. It could be used of an ambassador or official delegate. In the New Testament it is sometimes used specifically of Jesus' inner circle of twelve; but Paul sees not only himself but several others outside the Twelve as 'apostles', the criterion being whether the person had personally seen the risen Jesus. Jesus' own choice of twelve close associates symbolized his plan to renew God's people, Israel (who traditionally thought of themselves as having twelve tribes); after the death of Judas Iscariot (Matthew 27.5; Acts 1.18) Matthias was chosen by lot to take his place, preserving the symbolic meaning. During Jesus' lifetime they, and many other followers, were seen as his 'disciples', which means 'pupils' or 'apprentices'.

baptism

Literally, 'plunging' people into water. From within a wider Jewish tradition of ritual washings and bathings, **John the Baptist** undertook a vocation of baptizing people in the Jordan, not as one ritual among others but as a unique moment of repentance, preparing them for the coming of the **kingdom of God.** Jesus himself was baptized by John, identifying himself with this renewal movement and developing it in his own way. His followers in turn baptized others. After his **resurrection**, and the sending of the **holy spirit**, baptism became the normal sign and means of entry into the community of Jesus' people. As early as Paul it was aligned both with the **Exodus** from Egypt (1 Corinthians 10.2) and with Jesus' death and resurrection (Romans 6.2–11).

Christ, *see* **Messiah**

circumcision

The cutting off of the foreskin. Male circumcision was a major mark of identity for Jews, following its initial commandment to Abraham (Genesis 17), reinforced by Joshua (Joshua 5.2–9). Other peoples, e.g. the Egyptians, also circumcised male children. A line of thought from Deuteronomy (e.g. 30.6), through Jeremiah (e.g. 31.33), to the **Dead Sea Scrolls** and the New Testament (e.g. Romans 2.29) speaks of 'circumcision of the heart' as God's real desire, by which one may become inwardly what the male Jew is outwardly, that is, marked out as part of God's people. At periods of Jewish assimilation into the surrounding culture, some Jews tried to remove the marks of circumcision (e.g. 1 Maccabees 1.11–15).

covenant

At the heart of Jewish belief is the conviction that the one God, YHWH, who had made the whole world, had called Abraham and his family to belong to him in a special way. The promises God made to Abraham and his family, and the requirements that were laid on them as a result, came to be seen in terms either of the agreement that a king would make with a subject people, or of the marriage bond between husband and wife. One regular way of describing this relationship was 'covenant', which can thus include both promise and law. The covenant was renewed at Mount Sinai with the giving of the **Torah**; in Deuteronomy before the entry to the promised land; and, in a more focused way, with David (e.g. Psalm 89). Jeremiah 31 promised that after the punishment of **exile** God would make a 'new covenant' with his people, forgiving them and binding them to him more intimately. Jesus believed that this was coming true through his **kingdom**-proclamation and his death and **resurrection**. The early Christians developed these ideas in various ways, believing that in Jesus the promises had at last been fulfilled.

David's son, *see* **son of David**

Dead Sea Scrolls

A collection of texts, some in remarkably good repair, some extremely fragmentary, found in the late 1940s around Qumran (near the north-east corner of the Dead Sea), and virtually all now edited, translated and in the public domain. They formed all or part of the library of a strict monastic group, most likely Essenes, founded in the mid-second century BC and lasting until the Jewish–Roman war of AD 66–70. The scrolls include the earliest existing manuscripts of the Hebrew and Aramaic scriptures, and several other important documents of community regulations, scriptural exegesis, hymns, wisdom writings, and other literature. They shed a flood of light on one small segment within the Judaism of Jesus' day, helping us to understand how some Jews at least were thinking, praying and reading scripture. Despite attempts to prove the contrary, they make no reference to **John the Baptist**, Jesus, Paul, James or early Christianity in general.

demons, *see* **the satan**

disciple, *see* **apostle**

Essenes, *see* **Dead Sea Scrolls**

eternal life, *see* **present age**

eucharist

The meal in which the earliest Christians, and Christians ever since, obeyed Jesus' command to 'do this in remembrance of him' at the Last Supper (Luke 22.19; 1 Corinthians 11.23–26). The word 'eucharist' itself comes from the Greek for 'thanksgiving'; it means, basically, 'the thank-you meal', and looks back to the many times when Jesus took bread, gave thanks for it, broke it, and gave it to people (e.g. Luke 24.30; John 6.11). Other early phrases for the same meal are 'the Lord's supper' (1 Corinthians 11.20) and 'the breaking of bread' (Acts 2.42). Later it came to be called 'the Mass' (from the Latin word at the end of the service, meaning 'sent out') and 'Holy Communion' (Paul speaks of 'sharing' or 'communion' in the body and blood of Christ). Later theological controversies about the precise meaning of the various actions and elements of the meal should not obscure its centrality in earliest Christian living and its continuing vital importance today.

exile

Deuteronomy (29—30) warned that if Israel disobeyed YHWH, he would send his people into exile, but that if they then repented he would bring them back. When the Babylonians sacked Jerusalem and took the people into exile, prophets such as Jeremiah interpreted this as the fulfilment of this prophecy, and made further promises about how long exile would last (70 years, according to Jeremiah 25.12; 29.10). Sure enough, exiles began to return in the late sixth century BC (Ezra 1.1). However, the post-exilic period was largely a disappointment, since the people were still enslaved to foreigners (Nehemiah 9.36); and at the height of persecution by the Syrians Daniel 9.2, 24 spoke of the 'real' exile lasting not for 70 years but for 70 *weeks* of years, i.e. 490 years. Longing for the real 'return from exile', when the prophecies of Isaiah, Jeremiah, etc. would be fulfilled, and redemption from pagan oppression accomplished, continued to characterize many Jewish movements, and was a major theme in Jesus' proclamation and his summons to **repentance**.

Exodus

The Exodus from Egypt took place, according to the book of that name, under the leadership of Moses, after long years in which the Israelites had been enslaved there. (According to Genesis 15.13f., this was itself part of God's covenanted promise to Abraham.) It demonstrated, to them and to Pharaoh, King of Egypt, that Israel was God's special child (Exodus 4.22). They then wandered through the Sinai wilderness for 40 years, led by God in a pillar of cloud and fire; early on in this time they were given the **Torah** on Mount Sinai itself. Finally, after the death of Moses and under the leadership of Joshua, they crossed the Jordan and entered, and eventually conquered, the promised land of Canaan. This event, commemorated annually in Passover and other Jewish festivals, gave the Israelites not only a powerful memory of what had made them a people, but also a particular shape and content to their **faith** in YHWH as not only creator but also redeemer; and in subsequent enslavements, particularly the **exile**, they looked for a further redemption which would be, in effect, a new Exodus. Probably no other past event so dominated the imagination of first-century Jews; among them the early Christians, following the lead of Jesus himself, continually referred back to the Exodus to give

214

meaning and shape to their own critical events, most particularly Jesus' death and **resurrection**.

faith

Faith in the New Testament covers a wide area of human trust and trustworthiness, merging into love at one end of the scale and loyalty at the other. Within Jewish and Christian thinking faith in God also includes *belief*, accepting certain things as true about God, and what he has done in the world (e.g. bringing Israel out of Egypt; raising Jesus from the dead). For Jesus, 'faith' often seems to mean 'recognizing that God is decisively at work to bring the **kingdom** through Jesus'. For Paul, 'faith' is both the specific belief that Jesus is Lord and that God raised him from the dead (Romans 10.9) and the response of grateful human love to sovereign divine love (Galatians 2.20). This faith is, for Paul, the solitary badge of membership in God's people in **Christ**, marking them out in a way that **Torah**, and the works it prescribes, can never do.

Gentiles

The Jews divided the world into Jews and non-Jews. The Hebrew word for non-Jews, *goyim*, carries overtones both of family identity (i.e. not of Jewish ancestry) and of worship (i.e. of idols, not of the one true God **YHWH**). Though many Jews established good relations with Gentiles, not least in the Jewish Diaspora (the dispersion of Jews away from Palestine), officially there were taboos against contact such as intermarriage. In the New Testament the Greek word *ethne*, 'nations', carries the same meanings as *goyim*. Part of Paul's overmastering agenda was to insist that Gentiles who believed in Jesus had full rights in the Christian community alongside believing Jews, without having to become **circumcised**.

Gehenna, hell

Gehenna is, literally, the valley of Hinnom, on the south-west slopes of Jerusalem. From ancient times it was used as a garbage dump, smouldering with a continual fire. Already by the time of Jesus some Jews used it as an image for the place of punishment after death. Jesus' own usage blends the two meanings in his warnings both to Jerusalem itself (unless it repents, the whole city will become a smouldering heap of garbage) and to people in general (to beware of God's final judgment).

good news, gospel, message, word

The idea of 'good news', for which an older English word is 'gospel', had two principal meanings for first-century Jews. First, with roots in Isaiah, it meant the news of YHWH's long-awaited victory over evil and rescue of his people. Second, it was used in the Roman world for the accession, or birthday, of the emperor. Since for Jesus and Paul the announcement of God's inbreaking **kingdom** was both the fulfilment of prophecy and a challenge to the world's present rulers, 'gospel' became an important shorthand for both the message of Jesus himself and the apostolic message about him. Paul saw this message as itself the vehicle of God's saving power (Romans 1.16; 1 Thessalonians 2.13).

The four canonical 'gospels' tell the story of Jesus in such a way as to bring out both these aspects (unlike some other so-called 'gospels' circulated in the second and subsequent centuries, which tended both to cut off the scriptural and Jewish roots of Jesus' achievement and to inculcate a private spirituality rather than confrontation with the world's rulers). Since in Isaiah this creative, life-giving good news was seen as God's own powerful word (40.8; 55.11), the early Christians could use 'word' or 'message' as another shorthand for the basic Christian proclamation.

gospel, *see* good news

heaven

Heaven is God's dimension of the created order (Genesis 1.1; Psalm 115.16; Matthew 6.9), whereas 'earth' is the world of space, time and matter that we know. 'Heaven' thus sometimes stands, reverentially, for 'God' (as in Matthew's regular '**kingdom** of heaven'). Normally hidden from human sight, heaven is occasionally revealed or unveiled so that people can see God's dimension of ordinary life (e.g. 2 Kings 6.17; Revelation 1, 4—5). Heaven in the New Testament is thus not usually seen as the place where God's people go after death; at the end, the New Jerusalem descends *from* heaven *to* earth, joining the two dimensions for ever. 'Entering the kingdom of heaven' does not mean 'going to heaven after death', but belonging in the present to the people who steer their earthly course by the standards and purposes of heaven (cf. the Lord's Prayer: 'on earth as in heaven', Matthew 6. 10), and who are assured of membership in the **age to come**.

hell, *see* **Gehenna**

high priest, *see* **priest**

holy spirit

In Genesis 1.2, the spirit is God's presence and power *within* creation, without God being identified with creation. The same spirit entered people, notably the prophets, enabling them to speak and act for God. At his baptism by **John**, Jesus was specially equipped with the spirit, resulting in his remarkable public career (Acts 10.38). After his **resurrection**, his followers were themselves filled (Acts 2) by the same spirit, now identified as Jesus' own spirit: the creator God was acting afresh, remaking the world and them too. The spirit enabled them to live out a holiness which the **Torah** could not, producing 'fruit' in their lives, giving them 'gifts' with which to serve God, the world, and the church, and assuring them of future **resurrection** (Romans 8; Galatians 4—5; 1 Corinthians 12—14). From very early in Christianity (e.g. Galatians 4.1–7), the spirit became part of the new revolutionary definition of God himself: 'the one who sends the son and the spirit of the son'.

John (the Baptist)

Jesus' cousin on his mother's side, born a few months before Jesus; his father was a **priest**. He acted as a prophet, baptizing in the Jordan – dramatically re-enacting the **Exodus** from Egypt – to prepare people, by **repentance**, for God's coming judgment. He may have had some contact with the **Essenes**, though his eventual public message was different from theirs. Jesus' own vocation was decisively confirmed at his **baptism** by John. As part of John's message of the **kingdom**, he outspokenly criticized Herod Antipas for marrying his brother's wife. Herod had him imprisoned, and then beheaded him at his wife's request (Mark 6.14–29). Groups of John's disciples continued a separate existence, without merging into Christianity, for some time afterwards (e.g. Acts 19.1–7).

kingdom of God, kingdom of heaven

Best understood as the king*ship*, or sovereign and saving rule, of Israel's God YHWH, as celebrated in several Psalms (e.g. 99.1) and prophecies (e.g. Daniel 6.26–7). Because YHWH was the creator God, when he finally became king in the way he intended this would involve setting the world to rights, and particularly rescuing Israel from its enemies. 'Kingdom of God' and various equivalents (e.g. 'No king but God!') became revolutionary slogans around the time of Jesus. Jesus' own announcement of God's kingdom redefined these expectations around his own very different plan and vocation. His invitation to people to 'enter' the kingdom was a way of summoning them to allegiance to himself and his programme, seen as the start of God's long-awaited saving reign. For Jesus, the kingdom was coming not in a single move, but in stages, of which his own public career was one, his death and **resurrection** another, and a still future consummation another. Note that 'kingdom of **heaven**' is Matthew's preferred form for the same phrase, following a regular Jewish practice of saying 'heaven' rather than 'God'. It does not refer to a place ('heaven'), but to the fact of God's becoming king in and through Jesus and his achievement. Paul speaks of Jesus, as **Messiah**, already in possession of his kingdom, waiting to hand it over finally to the father (1 Corinthians 15.23–8; cf. Ephesians 5.5).

law, *see* Torah

legal experts, *see* Pharisees

leper, leprosy

In a world without modern medicine, tight medical controls were needed to prevent the spread of contagious diseases. Several such conditions, mostly severe skin problems, were referred to as 'leprosy', and two long biblical chapters (Leviticus 13—14) are devoted to diagnosis and prevention of it. Sufferers had to live away from towns and shout 'unclean' to warn others not to approach them (13.45). If they were healed, this had to be certified by a **priest** (14.2–32).

life, soul, spirit

Ancient people held many different views about what made human beings the special creatures they are. Some, including many Jews, believed that to be complete, humans needed bodies as well as inner selves. Others, including many influenced by the philosophy of Plato (fourth century BC), believed that the important part of a human was the 'soul' (Gk: *psyche*), which at death would be happily freed from its bodily prison. Confusingly for us, the same word *psyche* is often used in the New Testament within a Jewish framework where it clearly means 'life' or 'true self', without implying a body/soul dualism that devalues the body. Human inwardness of experience and understanding can also be referred to as 'spirit'. *See also* **holy spirit**; **resurrection**.

message, *see* **good news**

Messiah

The Hebrew word means literally 'anointed one', hence in theory either a prophet, **priest** or king. In Greek this translates as *Christos*; 'Christ' in early Christianity was a title, and only gradually became an alternative proper name for Jesus. In practice 'Messiah' is mostly restricted to the notion, which took various forms in ancient Judaism, of the coming king who would be David's true heir, through whom YHWH would rescue Israel from pagan enemies. There was no single template of expectations. Scriptural stories and promises contributed to different ideals and movements, often focused on (a) decisive military defeat of Israel's enemies and (b) rebuilding or cleansing the **Temple**. The **Dead Sea Scrolls** speak of two 'Messiahs', one a priest and the other a king. The universal early Christian belief that Jesus was Messiah is only explicable, granted his crucifixion by the Romans (which would have been seen as a clear sign that he was not the Messiah), by their belief that God had raised him from the dead, so vindicating the implicit messianic claims of his earlier ministry.

miracles

Like some of the old prophets, notably Elijah and Elisha, Jesus performed many deeds of remarkable power, particularly healings. The **gospels** refer to these as 'deeds of power', 'signs', 'marvels', or 'paradoxes'. Our word 'miracle' tends to imply that God, normally 'outside' the closed system of the world, sometimes 'intervenes'; miracles have then frequently been denied by sceptics as a matter of principle. However, in the Bible God is always present, however strangely, and 'deeds of power' are seen as *special* acts of a *present* God rather than as *intrusive* acts of an *absent* one. Jesus' own 'mighty works' are seen particularly, following prophecy, as evidence of his messiahship (e.g. Matthew 11.2–6).

Mishnah

The main codification of Jewish law (**Torah**) by the **rabbis**, produced in about AD 200, reducing to writing the 'oral Torah' which in Jesus' day ran parallel to the 'written Torah'. The Mishnah is itself the basis of the much larger collections of traditions in the two Talmuds (roughly AD 400).

parables

From the Old Testament onwards, prophets and other teachers used various story-telling devices as vehicles for their challenge to Israel (e.g. 2 Samuel 12.1–7). Sometimes these appeared as visions with interpretations (e.g. Daniel 7). Similar techniques were used by the **rabbis**. Jesus made his own creative adaptation of these traditions, in order to break open the world-view of his contemporaries and to invite them to share his vision of God's **kingdom** instead. His stories portrayed this as something that was *happening*, not just a timeless truth, and enabled his hearers to step inside the story and make it their own. As with some Old Testament visions, some of Jesus' parables have their own interpretations (e.g. the sower, Mark 4); others are thinly disguised retellings of the prophetic story of Israel (e.g. the wicked tenants, Mark 12).

parousia

Literally, it means 'presence', as opposed to 'absence', and sometimes used by Paul with this sense (e.g. Philippians 2.12). It was already used in the Roman world for the ceremonial arrival of, for example, the emperor at a subject city or colony. Although the ascended Lord is not 'absent' from the church, when he 'appears' (Colossians 3.4; 1 John 3.2) in his 'second coming' this will be, in effect, an 'arrival' like that of the emperor, and Paul uses it thus in 1 Corinthians 15.23; 1 Thessalonians 2.19; etc. In the **gospels** it is found only in Matthew 24 (verses 3, 27, 39).

Pharisees, legal experts, rabbis

The Pharisees were an unofficial but powerful Jewish pressure group through most of the first centuries BC and AD. Largely lay-led, though including some **priests**, their aim was to purify Israel through intensified observance of the Jewish law (**Torah**), developing their own traditions about the precise meaning and application of scripture, their own patterns of prayer and other devotion, and their own calculations of the national hope. Though not all legal experts were Pharisees, most Pharisees were thus legal experts.

They effected a democratization of Israel's life, since for them the study and practice of Torah was equivalent to worshipping in the **Temple** – though they were adamant in pressing their own rules for the Temple liturgy on an unwilling (and often Sadducean) priesthood. This enabled them to survive AD 70 and, merging into the early Rabbinic movement, to develop new ways forward. Politically they stood up for ancestral traditions, and were at the forefront of various movements of revolt against both pagan overlordship and compromised Jewish leaders. By Jesus' day there were two distinct schools, the stricter one of Shammai, more inclined towards armed revolt, and the more lenient one of Hillel, ready to live and let live.

Jesus' debates with the Pharisees are at least as much a matter of agenda and policy (Jesus strongly opposed their separatist nationalism) as about details of theology and piety. Saul of Tarsus was a fervent right-wing Pharisee, presumably a Shammaite, until his conversion.

After the disastrous war of AD 66–70, these schools of Hillel and Shammai continued bitter debate on appropriate policy. Following the further disaster of AD 135 (the failed Bar-Kochba revolt against Rome) their traditions were carried on by the rabbis who, though looking to the earlier Pharisees for inspiration, developed a Torah-piety in which personal holiness and purity took the place of political agendas.

present age, age to come, eternal life

By the time of Jesus many Jewish thinkers divided history into two periods: 'the present age' and 'the age to come' – the latter being the time when **YHWH** would at last act decisively to judge evil, to rescue Israel, and to create a new world of justice and peace. The early Christians believed that, though the full blessings of the coming age lay still in the future, it had already begun with Jesus, particularly with his death and **resurrection**, and that by **faith** and **baptism** they were able to enter it already. 'Eternal life' does not mean simply 'existence continuing without end', but 'the life of the age to come'.

priests, high priest

Aaron, the older brother of Moses, was appointed Israel's first high priest (Exodus 28—29), and in theory his descendants were Israel's priests thereafter. Other members of his tribe (Levi) were 'Levites', performing other liturgical duties but not sacrificing. Priests lived among the people all around the country, having a local teaching role (Leviticus 10.11; Malachi 2.7), and going to Jerusalem by rotation to perform the **Temple** liturgy (e.g. Luke 2.8).

David appointed Zadok (whose Aaronic ancestry is sometimes questioned) as high priest, and his family remained thereafter the senior priests in Jerusalem, probably the ancestors of the **Sadducees**. One explanation of the origins of the Qumran **Essenes** is that they were a dissident group who believed themselves to be the rightful chief priests.

rabbis, *see* Pharisees

repentance

Literally, this means 'turning back'. It is widely used in Old Testament and subsequent Jewish literature to indicate both a personal turning away from sin and Israel's corporate turning away from idolatry and back to YHWH. Through both meanings, it is linked to the idea of 'return from **exile**'; if Israel is to 'return' in all senses, it must 'return' to YHWH. This is at the heart of the summons of both **John the Baptist** and Jesus. In Paul's writings it is mostly used for **Gentiles** turning away from idols to serve the true God; also for sinning Christians who need to return to Jesus.

resurrection

In most biblical thought, human bodies matter and are not merely disposable prisons for the **soul**. When ancient Israelites wrestled with the goodness and justice of YHWH, the creator, they ultimately came to insist that he must raise the dead (Isaiah 26.19; Daniel 12.2–3) – a suggestion firmly resisted by classical pagan thought. The longed-for return from **exile** was also spoken of in terms of YHWH raising dry bones to new life (Ezekiel 37.1–14). These ideas were developed in the second-Temple period, not least at times of martyrdom (e.g. 2 Maccabees 7). Resurrection was not just 'life after death', but a newly embodied life *after* 'life after death'; those at present dead were either 'asleep', or seen as 'souls', 'angels' or 'spirits', awaiting new embodiment.

The early Christian belief that Jesus had been raised from the dead was not that he had 'gone to **heaven**', or that he had been 'exalted', or was 'divine'; they believed all those as well, but each could have been expressed without mention of resurrection. Only the bodily resurrection of Jesus explains the rise of the early church, particularly its belief in Jesus' messiahship (which his crucifixion would have called into question). The early Christians believed that they themselves would be raised to a new, transformed bodily life at the time of the Lord's return or **parousia** (e.g. Philippians 3.20f.).

sabbath

The Jewish sabbath, the seventh day of the week, was a regular reminder both of creation (Genesis 2.3; Exodus 20.8–11) and of the **Exodus** (Deuteronomy 5.15). Along with **circumcision** and the food laws, it was one of the badges of Jewish identity within the pagan world of late antiquity, and a considerable body of Jewish law and custom grew up around its observance.

sacrifice

Like all ancient people, the Israelites offered animal and vegetable sacrifices to their God. Unlike others, they possessed a highly detailed written code (mostly in Leviticus) for what to offer and how to offer it; this in turn was developed in the **Mishnah** (*c.* AD 200). The Old Testament specifies that sacrifices can only be offered in the Jerusalem **Temple**; after this was destroyed in AD 70, sacrifices ceased, and Judaism developed further the idea, already present in some teachings, of prayer, fasting and almsgiving as alternative forms of sacrifice. The early Christians used the language of sacrifice in connection with such things as holiness, evangelism and the **eucharist**.

Sadducees

By Jesus' day, the Sadducees were the aristocracy of Judaism, possibly tracing their origins to the family of Zadok, David's **high priest**. Based in Jerusalem, and including most of the leading priestly families, they had their own traditions and attempted to resist the pressure of the **Pharisees** to conform to theirs. They claimed to rely only on the Pentateuch (the first five books of the Old Testament), and denied any doctrine of a future life, particularly of the **resurrection** and other ideas associated with it, presumably because of the encouragement such beliefs gave to revolutionary movements. No writings from the Sadducees have survived, unless the apocryphal book of Ben-Sirach (Ecclesiasticus) comes from them. The Sadducees themselves did not survive the destruction of Jerusalem and the **Temple** in AD 70.

the satan, 'the accuser', demons

The Bible is never very precise about the identity of the figure known as 'the satan'. The Hebrew word means 'the accuser', and at times the satan seems to be a member of YHWH's heavenly council, with special responsibility as director of prosecutions (1 Chronicles 21.1; Job 1—2; Zechariah 3.1f.). However, it becomes identified variously with the serpent of the garden of Eden (Genesis 3.1–15) and with the rebellious daystar cast out of **heaven** (Isaiah 14.12–15), and was seen by many Jews as the quasi-personal source of evil standing behind both human wickedness and large-scale injustice, sometimes operating through semi-independent 'demons'. By Jesus' time various words were used to denote this figure, including Beelzebul/b (lit. 'Lord of the flies') and simply 'the evil one'; Jesus warned his followers against the deceits this figure could perpetrate. His opponents accused him of being in league with the satan, but the early Christians believed that Jesus in fact defeated it both in his own struggles with temptation (Matthew 4; Luke 4), his exorcisms of demons, and his death (1 Corinthians 2.8; Colossians 2.15). Final victory over this ultimate enemy is thus assured (Revelation 20), though the struggle can still be fierce for Christians (Ephesians 6.10–20).

scribes

In a world where many could not write, or not very well, a trained class of writers ('scribes') performed the important function of drawing up contracts for business, marriage, etc. Many scribes would thus be legal experts, and quite possibly **Pharisees**, though being a scribe was compatible with various political and religious standpoints. The work of Christian scribes was of initial importance in copying early Christian writings, particularly the stories about Jesus.

son of God

Originally a title for Israel (Exodus 4.22) and the Davidic king (Psalm 2.7); also used of ancient angelic figures (Genesis 6.2). By the New Testament period it was already used as a **messianic** title, for example, in the **Dead Sea Scrolls**. There, and when used of Jesus in the **gospels** (e.g. Matthew 16.16), it means, or reinforces, 'Messiah', without the later significance of 'divine'. However, already in Paul the transition to the fuller meaning (one who was already equal with God and was sent by him to become human and to become Messiah) is apparent, without loss of the meaning 'Messiah' itself (e.g. Galatians 4.4).

son of David

An alternative, and infrequently used, title for **Messiah**. The messianic promises of the Old Testament often focus specifically on David's son, for example 2 Samuel 7.12–16; Psalm 89.19–37. Joseph, Mary's husband, is called 'son of David' by the angel in Matthew 1.20.

son of man

In Hebrew or Aramaic, this simply means 'mortal', or 'human being'; in later Judaism, it is sometimes used to mean 'I' or 'someone like me'. In the New Testament the phrase is frequently linked to Daniel 7.13, where 'one like a son of man' is brought on the clouds of **heaven** to 'the Ancient of Days', being vindicated after a period of suffering, and is given kingly power. Though Daniel 7 itself interprets this as code for 'the people of the saints of the Most High', by the first century some Jews understood it as a **messianic** promise. Jesus developed this in his own way in certain key sayings which are best understood as promises that God would vindicate him, and judge those who had opposed him, after his own suffering (e.g. Mark 14.62). Jesus was thus able to use the phrase as a cryptic self-designation, hinting at his coming suffering, his vindication, and his God-given authority.

soul, *see* life

spirit, *see* **life, holy spirit**

Temple

The Temple in Jerusalem was planned by David (*c.* 1000 BC) and built by his son Solomon as the central sanctuary for all Israel. After reforms under Hezekiah and Josiah in the seventh century BC, it was destroyed by Babylon in 587 BC. Rebuilding by the returned **exiles** began in 538 BC, and was completed in 516, initiating the 'second-Temple period'. Judas Maccabaeus cleansed it in 164 BC after its desecration by Antiochus Epiphanes (167). Herod the Great began to rebuild and beautify it in 19 BC; the work was completed in AD 63. The Temple was destroyed by the Romans in AD 70. Many Jews believed it should and would be rebuilt; some still do. The Temple was not only the place of **sacrifice**; it was believed to be the unique dwelling of YHWH on earth, the place where **heaven** and earth met.

Torah, law

'Torah', narrowly conceived, consists of the first five books of the Old Testament, the 'five books of Moses' or 'Pentateuch'. (These contain much law, but also much narrative.) It can also be used for the whole Old Testament scriptures, though strictly these are the 'Law, prophets and writings'. In a broader sense, it refers to the whole developing corpus of Jewish legal tradition, written and oral; the oral Torah was initially codified in the **Mishnah** around AD 200, with wider developments found in the two Talmuds, of Babylon and Jerusalem, codified around AD 400. Many Jews in the time of Jesus and Paul regarded the Torah as being so strongly God-given as to be almost itself, in some sense, divine; some (e.g. Ben-Sirach 24) identified it with the figure of 'Wisdom'. Doing what Torah said was not seen as a means of earning God's favour, but rather of expressing gratitude, and as a key badge of Jewish identity.

the Twelve, *see* **apostle**

Word, *see also* **good news**

YHWH

The ancient Israelite name for God, from at least the time of the